CHURCH FIGHTS

CHURCH FIGHTS

Managing Conflict in the Local Church

by Speed Leas
and Paul Kittlaus

THE WESTMINSTER PRESS · PHILADELPHIA

PUBLISHED BY THE WESTMINSTER PRESS ®
PHILADELPHIA, PENNSYLVANIA

PRINTED IN THE UNITED STATES OF AMERICA

---

9   8   7   6   5   4

Library of Congress Cataloging in Publication Data

Leas, Speed, 1937–
  Church fights.

  Bibliography: p.
  1. Church management.   2. Conflict (Psychology)
I. Kittlaus, Paul, 1934–   joint author.   II.   Title.
BV652.L39   253   73-6790
ISBN 0-664-24974-4

To Connie and Genie

I am sure we can begin by agreeing
that every major advance in
civilization has resulted from conflict.
ROSS STAGNER

Contents

Preface

This book represents the personal experience and reflection of the authors. We have been engaged for five years as consultants to churches and other organizations that have been involved in conflicts of one kind or another and have applied the discipline of Action/Reflection which we learned as Action Trainers in COMMIT, the Action Training Center in Los Angeles.

This book is a synthesis of our study of the literature related to the behavioral sciences, conflict, and management, the training we received from other professionals in the field, our experience in local churches as pastor, as trainer, and as consultant, and of our reflection on this experience, training, and reading. It is meant to be a manual for the individual who wants to do something to help his church, not to be a reflection piece or a contribution to the development of the theory of conflict management.

The structure of the book is meant to be like a repairman's manual. It is expected that the reader is someone with a conflict that he wants to do something

about. One may read the book from beginning to end
to get a feel for the proper sequence of events to properly
manage a conflict, or he may read one chapter or another
to find material relevant to the particular stage of the
conflict that he happens to be experiencing. The chart
in Chapter 3 is meant to be a map to help one find his
way through the book and through a conflict situation
that he may be having in his local church or other voluntary association.

We would like to acknowledge the help that certain
individuals gave in making this book possible in its
present form. Rev. Bill Moremen, Ms. Elizabeth Regis-
ter, and Rev. Tilden Edwards were very helpful in their
encouragement and their critical reading of early drafts
of the manuscript. Especially important to us in the
preparation of the book was Dr. Joseph Hough, of the
School of Theology at Claremont. When we asked him
to look over our work he spent many hours carefully
reading the text and making numerous suggestions for
its improvement. Joe's thoughtful reviewing, his support,
encouragement, and friendship, were uniquely important
to us in the preparation of this material. Finally, we
would like to thank the Board of Directors of COMMIT
who gave us the time and freedom to do this in addition
to our regular consulting and training work.

SPEED LEAS
PAUL KITTLAUS

1

Introduction

Current polarization in the church will no doubt get worse before it gets better. The gap gets wider and wider between those who want the church involved in the issues of the day and those who cherish the traditional forms and formulations. Conflict of this kind is not unhealthy if it is in the service of the church's ministry and mission, but the contemporary conflict has now advanced until it is not grounded in our ministry but in the defense of positions. Its mood is not one of fidelity to our mission but one of distrust and acrimony.

This study addresses itself to this unfortunate and unhealthy polarization.[1]

This statement by an Old Testament professor recognizes the contemporary plight of the church as one of conflict, and understands the struggle as an urgent one, a struggle in which not only the identity of the church is at stake but also its whole life.

We quote Professor Brueggemann because we sense ouselves to be in the same plight as he. We care for the church. We see its survival in terms of its ministry and

mission. We bring to the struggle different skills and a
different theoretical base but sense the same struggle
and seek the same goal: a healthy church in mission.
Here we will attempt to mobilize our resources to address this unfortunate and unhealthy polarization, using
the theory and skills of applied behavioral science and
the combined experience of twenty years of professional
ministry with local churches.

What Is the Problem?

This book is written for churches whose leadership
and membership is immobilizing itself and not fulfilling
its mission because of disintegrating, dysfunctional, and
dissociating conflicts: "disintegrating," where the church
is using up its resources (losing members, money, and
energy) on unhealthy conflict; "dysfunctional," where
it is spending its energy on nonproductive issues; and
"dissociating," where it is experiencing the agony of
interpersonal hostility.

Some of the symptoms of the problems are:
  internal division
  parish members informally organizing cliques and
    factions
  increasing use of voting to make decisions
  long-drawn-out, personally unfulfilling meetings
  sharply increased attendance at certain meetings
  decreasing attendance over the long run
  increased use of hostile language
  experiencing other members as enemies
  feelings of fear that the organization is out of con-
    trol

win/lose attitudes in decision-making

people looking for conspiracies

conspiracies

increased discussion about the goals of the church
  indicating a breakdown of consensus

increased incongruity between what people say at
  meetings and what they say over the phone con-
  cerning church matters

unfocused anxiety and anger

displacement: people looking for reasons to disagree
  without naming (or sometimes without knowing)
  the "real" problem

acting out: overresponding or other incongruous behavior

blocks of pledges not being paid

members transferring membership

every issue at every meeting experienced as part of a
  larger struggle

communication patterns change

friendship patterns change

increasing mistrust of others

painful pressure on the minister, evidenced by increased use of the theme of reconciliation in sermons, prayers, and hymns

desperate "circuit-riding" calling by the minister,
  attempting to hold everything together

minister developing a sense of personal failure

job-hunting by the minister

These symptoms may be indicators of other problems
in the church, but after careful data gathering and analysis, we often find that it is the paralysis of poorly managed conflict which is producing one or more of these
behaviors. Sometimes we find that the conflict has been

generated and dealt with overtly, but more often than not, strategies are ingeniously invented to avoid conflict, having the effect of postponing it and making it more volatile and eventually more destructive. It is our thesis that inventiveness and creativity which have been focused on efforts to avoid conflict need now to be used in developing better processes for dealing with it.

THE PURPOSE OF THIS BOOK

This book is written for pastors and lay persons who are interested in applying the behavioral sciences to their churches. It is a book for those persons who are experiencing conflict and wish to develop strategies to manage it better. Specifically, our goal is to provide concepts, experiences, processes, and tools for congregational leaders desiring to lead a congregation through conflict in such a way that the conflict is useful to, and not detrimental to, the further development of the mission of the church.

SIDE EFFECTS THAT ARE NOT OUR GOALS

Although these pages may be useful to persons who seek the following as goals, we are clear that they are not adequate statements of the intention of this book. They do not sufficiently reflect the mission that we understand the church to share with the living God, but are nonetheless often used as criteria for determining success and failure of conflict management. The following therefore are *not* goals for this book:

to maintain the institution
to improve the psyche of the minister
to increase friendships
to raise the budget
to improve group process
to have a "successful" institution

We would hope that some of these goals might emerge as characteristics of a church that has managed conflict well, but they are not the primary goals of the material offered here. Our goal is to help the church to accomplish its mission.

ACTION TRAINING AND INSTITUTIONAL CHURCH MAINTENANCE

The authors of this book are full-time trainers and consultants with COMMIT (Center of Metropolitan Mission In-Service Training), an Action Training Center in Los Angeles. COMMIT was established originally to train church people committed to social change engagement with the urban world and as a resource to those community groups who see the resources of the church as useful to their struggle. Recently, however, we have been called upon with sharply increased frequency to come to the aid of congregations entangled in conflict. We have found that the skills and resources of Action Trainers are often relevant to church management as well as to social change. Where necessary, we have drawn on other management resources, and in some instances we have invented new ones.

To some persons this may seem to be merely institutional maintenance. It is becoming increasingly clear to us, however, that while planned change through engagement by clergy and laity in community, urban, and national issues is still crucial to our understanding of the mission of the church, another factor is just as important: the same forces at work challenging other institutions of the society are also challenging the institutional church. We see the cultural revolutions, the political changes, and the economic dynamics of our world as a challenge and an inspiration for us as Christians. We see these factors as the impetus for positive social change. They have challenged and impelled us to be involved in the world. Yet, within the institution that is our base of operation and resource, i.e., the church, these conflicts are often experienced as a threat, painfully forcing us to choose between entrenchment against change and willingness to change ourselves. Whereas we, as social change agents and actors, have been critical of our own institution for expending so many of its resources on itself, we now find it necessary to spend more of our resources on our own institution because of the forces of change at work on it. Therefore we have chosen to sharpen our base-building skills to make those skills available on both sides of the struggle, i.e., to the worldly mission of the church in social change ventures and in the struggle to maintain the institutional church as it confronts the new world and is confronted by it.

TYPOLOGY: CONGREGATIONAL STYLES

We have developed a typology to characterize a number of general models of congregational styles and goals.

It will be clear, within this typology, which churches are most likely to find our material most useful.

1. *The Shelter Community*
   a. *Characteristic Membership*

   The members are socially homogeneous—i.e., of similar racial and economic segments of the larger society. They get along easily and are comfortable with each other. They enjoy similar social events, such as church potlucks.

   b. *Pastor's Role*

   The pastor's role is largely person to person. This may be either in the counseling relationship or in the dynamic style of preaching for decision. High priority is put on his calling and his relating to the pastoral needs of each member.

   c. *Meaning of Key Language*

   (1) *Reconciliation* is largely defined as one's relationship as an individual to God.

   (2) *Mission* is defined as individual salvation and social service to individuals in economic, emotional, or other need.

   (3) *Evangelism* is defined as the saving of souls for Christ and as programs of gathering the saved into community.

   d. *Major Program Focus*

   Program is focused on the social and the spiritual needs of the members of the congregation.

2. *The Pluralistic Community*
   a. *Characteristic Membership*

   The membership is characterized by diversity—social, racial, political, and theological.

b. *Pastor's Role*

The pastor typically sees himself as neutral to the variety of heterogeneous interests in the church and as attempting to be helpful to all persons and groups. The pastoral director or executive role is often characteristic. If the membership is large enough for multiple staff, often a theologically and socially heterogeneous staff is called in order to appeal to diverse age groups and interest groups.

c. *Meaning of Key Language*

(1) *Reconciliation* is defined as the internal dynamics within the community of persons within the church. The focus is neighbor to neighbor in the pew. Becoming a model of a loving community is an important goal.

(2) *Mission* is defined as the effort to show forth a model of diverse people and groups in loving community. ("See those Christians, how they love one another.") The church becomes the model of the way the world should be.

(3) *Evangelism* is defined as the effort to bring balanced diversity into the fellowship.

d. *Major Program Emphasis*

Programming is a "something for everyone" effort. Diverse interests and groups require diversity in programming. Typically, much energy is needed to work on interpersonal and intergroup tensions within the fellowship, and training often is needed for interpersonal facilitation and conflict management.

3. *The Servant-Critic Community*
   a. *Characteristic Membership*

The members of this style of congregation are often politically homogeneous, reflecting the primary focus of this church on worldly issues. Typically, this congregation is the remnant of a larger congregation after a major conflict over a social issue. All the dynamics described later of typical positive and negative aspects of conflict in a group are often operative.

b. *Pastor's Role*

Usually the pastor is interested in prophetic involvement in the world's agenda. Often, for example, he is skilled in community organization and community development and involved in secular social change efforts.

c. *Meaning of Key Language*

(1) *Reconciliation* is defined as the work required to bridge the chasms that exist between groups in the world, e.g., between blacks and Anglos. Also it means identifying with the struggle of the poor and oppressed for a place of honor and dignity in the society.

(2) *Mission* means letting the suffering in the world write the agenda and it means pouring out the church's resources toward nonchurch peoples.

(3) *Evangelism* is defined as the congregation's witness in the public sector.

d. *Major Program Focus*

Programming usually is focused on involvement in major public issues. Both individuals and groups are giving leadership to community groups addressing issues, and frequently this church is working at getting its denomination to take a stand or use its resources to support the struggle of the oppressed.

It is the pluralistic model that contains the tendencies and dynamics most clearly akin to the material in this book. Those for whom the church is to be functionally heterogeneous in its membership and programmatically pluralistic will benefit most from this material on conflict management.

On the one hand, those congregations which seek to provide a shelter from the world, personal salvation in the form of decisions, Christianity under the charismatic leadership of a strong, dominating, evangelistic preacher may not find this material useful. We assume here lay involvement in policy formation for the congregation and, in this process, contending forces from lively, caring, involved persons who value a multifaceted congregational life.

On the other hand, those congregations in the prophetic servant-critic [2] model, with their worldly agenda, may find that this material assumes too much plurality for their work. We may seem to value a "something for everybody" approach which the servant-critics will find running counter to their more narrowly defined goals for social change. An experience that we have had illustrates this problem. One minister, after studying theology, sociology, social change theory, and experience in social change, developed a clear vision of the kind of church life required to address most effectively the "future shock" he experienced in his church. After the minister had shared his vision with the congregation, only a small number of the laity were convinced that his perception was accurate or his goals appropriate. He struggled to get his vision adopted in all forms of congregational life from worship to budgeting to church life-style. A fight developed when great resistances

to the pastor and his plans were generated. A contract
was developed which provided for us to intervene as a
third party. To this contract the pastor, *his* cadre, and
the "resisters" agreed. They covenanted to work together
through the process based upon the methodology included in this book. The end product, after a series of
meetings, was a new set of policies representing new
ideas and a stronger commitment of a much larger portion of the members to a new set of church goals (but
not necessarily the pastor's goals). The minister, upon
reflection, recognized that new strength had indeed
emerged from a broader base of the membership. Further, the new policies were more than mere compromise
between the two sides of the fight—the experience
had been synergistic in that totally new possibilities had
opened up when the two sides seriously worked together.
But the pastor still felt that the product was short of
what was finally required for the future church. He had
done his best to explore and share his vision with his
congregation under good conditions, and they had
agreed to only part of it. He now feels, from the van-
tage point of another ministry, that built into our process is a compromise solution which, in his opinion, may
not represent those dynamics which will thrust the
church into the new age.

We grant that this feeling may be an accurate reflection on the products of this style of conflict management. We are clearly not developing in this material a
program of the new church for the new age. That is
another task than the one addressed in this book, and
it is an important task. To bring into a church an alternative vision, there must be advocates and thus contestants, but well-managed conflict also requires a referee

3. For a theoretical discussion of social science models and their assumptions, see Gibson Winter, *Elements for a Social Ethic* (The Macmillan Company, 1968). Management theory is largely grounded in the functional social analysis of organizations.

2

Assumptions and Concepts About Conflict and Change

WHAT IS CONFLICT?

The Latin root of the word "conflict" reveals the essence of its meaning. The root word, *fligere*, means "to strike." This root is found in the word "inflict," which means to strike something onto (in) somebody, and in the word "profligate," which literally means to "strike forward" or to knock someone on the face. The word "conflict" means to "strike together," and it is this meaning which is fundamental to our working definition.

Conflict happens when two pieces of matter try to occupy the same space at the same time. The two pieces of matter attempting to enter the same space at the same time will conflict, or strike together. This analogy can be used in looking at conflicting goals of a group. Conflicting goals are two purposes or objectives that cannot occupy the same group at the same time. Or, as Ross Stagner says, conflict is "a situation in which two or more human beings desire goals which they perceive as being attainable by one or the other *but not by both.*" [1]

Another way to look at conflict is to see it as behavior that produces a barrier to another person's attempt to meet his needs. Conflict may arise because a father has the need to sit quietly at home in the evening after a hard day at work and his son (from any of a number of needs that he may have) decides to practice the electric guitar. The son's need to practice strikes against the father's need for quiet. The two needs cannot be met simultaneously under the same roof. That is conflict.

Or, one may think that the goal of the church is to provide a haven and a rest from the terrors of modern living and another may think that the church's purpose is to equip the soldiers of the Lord for battle in the world. The two goals strike together, each trying to push the other out. If the members of the church who held different ideas about what the church should be doing (or what its goals should be) did not care what the others' views were—or allowed the others to go their own way—there would be no conflict. For conflict to exist, each side (and there may be many sides) must see that the work of the other interferes with his own work: the ideas or the values or the actions must be attempting to occupy the same space at the same time.

KINDS OF CONFLICT

We can differentiate between three major ways in which conflict is experienced: intrapersonal, interpersonal, and substantive.

Intrapersonal Conflict

Intrapersonal conflict is that struggle which a person has within himself. It may be different feelings warring with each other, or it may be the struggle that one has in trying to determine whether he will protest the war in Southeast Asia by not paying the federal tax on his telephone bill or whether he will not take this action because it might threaten his credit rating or the security of his family. Intrapersonal conflict is the contest that one has with different parts of his self. One's puritan conscience can be in conflict with his playful side; or his rational, calculating self can be in contest with his love for the nonrational and aesthetic. This kind of conflict can affect church life when it spills over into church business, as when an individual sends conflicting messages about what he wants the church to be. For example, many people would prefer experimental, modern worship services but don't want to threaten or undermine others' needs for traditional forms. From the intrapersonal conflict ("I need more experimental worship" striking against "I need to help others get what they want in worship") come two different messages to the church: "Let's experiment with worship," and, on the other hand, "Let's not experiment with worship."

Interpersonal Conflict

Another kind of conflict that is often encountered in churches is interpersonal conflict. We mean by interpersonal conflict that which is related to differences between people but is not related primarily to issues. This is the conflict where one person is striking against the other primarily over their incompatibility as persons. This conflict is not generated by what a person does or what he thinks about an issue, but by how he feels about the other person.

Illustrative of this type of conflict are those situations where one is in conflict with another simply because the other is black, or old, or a minister, or a layman, or happens to be one with whom he has never gotten along. Not long ago we worked in a church-related agency where there was great conflict between the head of the agency and one of his staff persons. The staff member said that he and the director had never gotten along and that he resented having a boss. The director, on the other hand, didn't like his staff person and let few opportunities go by to needle or annoy him. This was primarily an interpersonal conflict because most of the issues were not substantive (over philosophy or competence) but were primarily related to individual feelings about another person.

Substantive Conflict

A third kind of conflict is substantive. Substantive conflict can be between two individuals, or between an individual and a group, or between groups. Substantive conflict has to do with conflict over facts, means, ends, or values. Between individuals it can be a contest between the chairman of the board of trustees and the minister over how to spend church dollars. It is the conflict between the choir director and the leader of the Boy Scout troop over who has title to the minister's parking space on Thursday nights. Substantive conflict between persons can be manifested in the life of the church if the two personalities in conflict seek to gain support from others for their positions. Or it can remain between the two parties only.

Often substantive conflict is between groups who have loyalty to their own group and position. This intergroup conflict is illustrated when factions develop over whether the minister ought to be asked to resign, or when the youth group confronts the deacons on their commitment to traditional worship forms.

The reason we have differentiated between these forms of conflict is that it is usually the case that different methods are appropriate for solving different kinds of conflict. This book will be addressing itself primarily to substantive conflict between individuals and groups. Intrapersonal conflict is best dealt with through personal counseling, therapy, study, or other methods directed at individual change. Interpersonal conflict can also be dealt with through therapy and counseling (e.g., marriage counseling) and through other methods such as confrontations, encounter groups, sensitivity training, and education. We will describe one method for dealing with interpersonal conflict later in the book.

Looking more closely at substantive conflict, we have followed Tannenbaum and Schmidt's [2] categories. They have distinguished four kinds of substantive conflict. The first is *conflict over the facts* of a situation. For example, some say that a particular church's membership is declining, whereas others say that it is increasing. This conflict can be settled by taking a census in the church to determine whether the membership has changed and how.

Another kind of substantive striking together can be *conflict over the methods, or means,* for achieving a solution to a problem. We may agree on the fact that the church's membership is declining, but our conflict may be over what we are going to do about it. One person may say that the pastor should not speak of controversial subjects from the pulpit (or pew, or choir room, or social hall), and another may say that it is precisely because the church has refused to take a stand that new persons are not attracted to the church. Or one may agree that the church should use its resources to assist victims of poverty to find dignity and freedom in this country, but there is contention as to which groups ought to receive funding from the church.

Conflict over ends, or goals, is also common. This is illustrated by the contest over what should be the purpose of the social action committee. In one church there was great controversy as to whether the social action committee should be a group whose task was to change the attitudes and beliefs of the congregation, or whether it should be an agent for change in the community outside the church. "What should be the purpose of this church?" is a question that is often heatedly debated in churches these days, and the outcome has direct bearing on the whole shape of the church's life.

Finally, there is *conflict over values*. The values question is different from the goals question in that it is the foundation upon which the goals are built. The answer to the goals question determines the direction that an organization will take, but the answer to the values question determines which goals will be chosen. In every social system there is a common body of values, beliefs, sentiments, etc., that are the criteria which determine the choices that are made with regard to ends and means. It is quite possible for a church to be in a quandary as to what its purpose should be and, at the same time, to have a consensus as to the underlying values relevant to the goal decisions.

We have experienced the situation where there is conflict with regard to goals, yet some persons in the church assume the situation to be a conflict of values. On examining the situation carefully, we find consensus as to the criteria for determining goals but conflict as to which goals will be chosen. An illustration for this is a church that was experiencing great pain over whether it should become involved in a current political issue. The situation was being argued as a goal question: Is it the purpose of the church to work for the resolution (reconciliation) of temporal issues? Some said that this was a value question. They maintained that people had very different operational values. However, as we looked into the matter, we found amazing congruence in the area of values. Everyone could agree that the church should be a community of people with diverse opinions; everyone has a right to and should be encouraged to express his opinion; there are some issues the church cannot be silent on (hunger and racism it was agreed in this church were evils to be eradicated). When the people came to see that there were so many areas of common agreement, their "enemies" seemed less foreboding, the hostilities were abated, and a problem-solving process was instituted to begin to work on the goal problem they were confronting: Shall we get involved in this particular temporal issue?

As a final word on our definition of conflict, it should be pointed out that we have not equated conflict with bad feelings, hostile attitudes, or anger. Bad feelings do not constitute interpersonal or substantive conflict until they are manifested in some kind of behavior that strikes against another person or group. Indeed, hostile sentiments do indicate a predisposition to engage in conflict, but until there is a striking together, for our purposes conflict does not exist. The number of areas where people are not satisfied and have hostile feelings is so vast—almost to the point of being infinite—that to attempt to deal with all the places where one has bad or hostile feelings would be to neglect the important tasks that one is given as a member of a Christian congregation. The fact is that until the hostile feelings are acted upon, they amount to what is primarily an intrapersonal problem and not an interpersonal or substantive conflict.

The Functions of Conflict

There are four major areas in the life of organizations and, especially of churches, where conflict plays an essentially positive role,[3] i.e., a role that is life-enhancing and helpful to group maintenance and mission accomplishment. This seems like a paradox: that something that can feel so bad can yet be of such importance to group life and so valuable to the accomplishment of mission. Nonetheless, the positive functions of conflict make it essential to healthy organizational life.

Empowerment

The first major positive function of conflict is that it energizes and gives empowerment to group life. Richard Walton had described the phenomenon of conflict's empowering qualities in showing that when the amount of threat, or tension, or anxiety in an organization is low "there is no sense of urgency, no necessity to look for alternative ways of behaving, and no incentive for conciliatory overtures." [4] In a marriage you might hear one of the partners saying that the other takes him or her for granted in this kind of situation. In a church the membership is described as apathetic. With no sense of dissatisfaction, with no vision of a better way to live or to do things, with no pain, there is very little chance that there will be any action.

Walton goes on to say that when the level of threat is higher—at a moderate level, for instance—"the person searches for and integrates more information, considers more alternatives, and experiences a higher sense of urgency in changing the situation." [5] This is the kind of circumstance where one must be on his toes. Here one is challenged and has to muster the skills, knowledge, and whatever other resources he has in order to stay on top of things. Here one is in a healthy competitive state where every idea is challenged, so only the best ideas are kept. Here the organization is constantly aware that it must do things as efficiently as possible, so that whatever is dying and has little value is sloughed off, and that whatever is living and bringing new life can be recognized, nurtured, and supported. A church that has a healthy amount of tension and conflict is one where programs and plans are challenged, so those which have greatest merit, value, and meaning to the mission of the church are implemented. It is a church where people have had a good deal of experience challenging each other around the substance of the church's life (not petty bickering and defamation of personalities), so that when a real, significant challenge or threat does come, the church is able to manage the conflict. On the basis of its established processes for managing conflict and its history that has confirmed in each person's mind an awareness that he will be able to weather the storm, the church can use the conflict for creative change. Those churches which have had little or no conflict and suddenly are confronted by it have little ability to stay strong and deal with the conflict creatively.[6]

Finally, there are situations where the level of conflict is more than the system can bear. In Walton's words: "At a very high level of threat the person's ability to process information and perceive alternatives decreases. This can produce rigidity of positions and polarization of adversaries." [7] A sign of conflict poorly managed can be seen when the antagonists do battle, not in terms of the current issue, but in terms of the historic commitments to "our side." Instead of asking the question, Which side of the issue should I be on this time? the question gets asked, Which way is my team going? I'll go with them right or wrong.

Where there is a very high level of threat, it is immobilizing and tends to produce shock in the organization rather than energizing it or challenging it to fulfill its mission. However, we must not lose sight of the fact that the level of threat for any given organization is a relative thing. For a church with a history of healthy conflict it would take an extreme threat indeed to weaken it. But a church that has had no such history, a church in which conflict is normally suppressed and avoided, may quickly feel that it has failed if anyone raises a question about its goals or procedures.

One church that normally suppressed conflict lost many of its members because the minister moved the pews at an angle to the Communion table rather than parallel to it. The shock of this unprecedented move was so great that the church fell apart. Attendance at worship and at church meetings declined. The atmosphere was cold, impersonal, and charged. People were suspicious of each other. Thus, what may have been experienced in some churches as an insignificant conflict can be experienced in other churches as overwhelming and devastating because of its history. Where the amount of conflict and tension is too high, it will be immobilizing. Instead of seeking ways to deal creatively with the problem, the people tend to be rigid, bureaucratic, and legalistic. They run to the bylaws and use them as a cudgel or shelter, depending on whichever seems appropriate.

The optimum situation in a local church, then, is not the absence of conflict, a situation where the church is apathetic and lacking in creativity, nor is it the situation where persons are continually bickering, and fighting, and attacking. Rather, conflict well used and managed is present and is handled to energize and mobilize the people to initiate action and respond to needs that they really care about in the church and its community.

Establishing Identity

The second thing that conflict can do is to help the group establish its identity and boundary lines. This is especially true when the group is involved in conflict with a group of "outsiders." The church has used conflict as a means of establishing its identity from its very inception: "He who is not with me is against me, and he who does not gather with me scatters" (Matt. 12:30). Obviously, Jesus was using conflict to differentiate between those who were in the "ingroup" and those who were in the "outgroup."

Controversy forces people to choose sides. And once a person has chosen sides, he is required to answer the question, What differentiates us from them? That which makes one group different from the other gives them, in part, their identity. In a recent church fight, the congregation was split over the kind of worship service that should be held on Sunday mornings: whether it should be traditional or experimental. For about a year this had been discusssed from the pulpit, in deacons meetings, in board meetings, at choir rehearsals, and at many other gatherings of church members. The way the issue was described in these conversations was that older members wanted traditional worship and younger members wanted experimental worship. When we were asked to help, one of the first things we had the people do was to declare whose side they were on, the traditionalists' or the experimenters'. We found that the two camps were highly heterogeneous with regard to age. All of a sudden both sides had to find new reasons for what split them and a new way to explain who they were. The discovery of these new reasons made it possible for each group to clarify its position, make a stronger case for it, and, finally, to offer more realistic alternatives to solve the problem.

In the predominantly white church, we are learning that as organized black groups make demands for greater participation in the church's life they become more and more clear as to who they are. Many whites then express their jealousy: "The blacks are more together than we are." This is another illustration of a group developing its identity through the use of conflict. In declaring that they are not white, blacks are affirming that their characteristics, unique culture, and style of doing things are good. This new identity means that blacks, therefore, negotiate from strength and a positive identity rather than from weakness and an uncertainty as to what the church needs to be and what their place will be in it.

Unifying the Ingroup

A third positive function of conflict is that it tends to unify the ingroup. In a conflict situation each contestant tends to play down the differences that exist within his own group and it becomes more effective as a task group. There is a negative side to this, however. The ingroup tends to let traditional leadership patterns dominate rather than to risk an "in-house" struggle and dissipating energy on the question of who would be the best leader at this time. The ingroup also tends to overlook its own inadequacies and see only the inadequacies of its opponent or opponents.

So when a church begins to polarize over an issue, we find that the various factions tend to operate fairly well as teams, though the whole organization may diminish in effectiveness. One church in Southern California gave its old parsonage to the youth group for their exclusive meetinghouse. The young people were very pleased with the gift and decided that it would be appropriate to symbolize their ownership of the building by painting a garish mural on the living room wall. In the ensuing battle over whether the youth could do any more painting in the building, the youth became a thriving and effective group and could see absolutely nothing wrong with their "creation." On the other hand, the official church boards gathered together to denounce the mural and could see nothing good about it. This temporary polarizing helped each side become more clear as to what it wanted in the church and made each side a better working unit than it had been. When we were called to the church we were able to help it see these good things which were coming out of the conflict as well as to develop strategies and policies for dealing with the struggle.

Bearing the Intolerable

Finally, conflict provides a means that makes it possible for us to bear otherwise intolerable circumstances. Conflict in itself can be a release, a means by which we are able to bring within the limits of toleration that which would otherwise be unbearable. One group of men in a particular denomination were outraged by their church's silence on the war in Southeast Asia. If it had not been possible for this group to confront its denomination, to make demands for change, and to try to organize churchmen to change their stand on this issue, these men would not have stayed in the church. The very fact that they could challenge, cajole, and threaten their denomination meant that they would stay there and give it their support in other areas of their common life together.

CONFLICT GONE AWRY

There are situations and times when conflict becomes too much to bear for the organization or for the in-

dividuals within it. But in our experience the fear of
conflict going awry, getting out of hand, of somebody
really getting hurt, is mostly a product of people's fantasies. In most situations church people are strong; they
can handle conflict and, in fact, enjoy challenging and
being challenged. It is the fear of what might happen
that gets in the way; it is blind obedience to the norm
(especially prevalent in churches) that conflict is wrong
or unchristian that sends individuals scurrying to the
woods when conflict may be imminent. The problem
with conflict, in most situations, is not that it will be
destructive of the group—probably just the opposite is
true—but its occurrence disregards the group norm that
conflict is a no-no. Persons who try to deal openly with
conflict are placed on the list of those to be avoided,
shunned, and cast out. In the minds of church members,
any conflict at all is conflict gone awry. This group norm
is highly debilitating to the life of the group because it
gets in the way of possibilities for growth, change, and
development.

We should not leave this issue without recognizing
that there are situations where conflict does lead to
violence, dissolution of the group, destruction of the
consensus, and/or control (defeat) of the minority by
the majority or vice versa. While these situations are not
uncommon, they tend to happen where the perceived
choices open to the group are either no conflict or all-
out war. Where a church has had a history of dealing
with conflicts (large and small), where it has a process
for dealing with them fairly and openly, and where the
membership is not immobilized by a difference of opinion, it is possible, even probable, that the parties involved
in the conflict will be able to choose behavior other than

search and destroy, as the only way to deal with the "enemy."

MISCELLANEOUS ASSUMPTIONS ABOUT CONFLICT

We would like to share some assumptions about conflict that will be relevant to choices of how, when, and where a person might be dealing with it in his church.

Conflict is possible where relationships are not tenuous. Where interpersonal relationships are not firm, where people don't know each other, where they have a minimum amount of trust, and little feeling for how others operate, the very strong tendency will be to suppress any conflict. On the other hand, when people care about one another and what the other does, then there can be conflict.

George Bach, in his book *The Intimate Enemy,* says that conflict is a function of caring: If one doesn't care about the other person or what he is doing, one will not be motivated to fight with him. If one doesn't care what other people are doing or saying within the church, one will not be interested in them and will avoid confronting them. To the extent that one does care about the other, and the relationship is significant, one will be able to be in conflict with the other. As Bach describes a marriage relationship: "To be of central significance to a partner means to be close . . . , to be included and brought into the private world of feelings, wants, and fears of the other; to care and fuss about the other's growth. . . . People are hungry for evidence that they are of central significance to an intimate partner. They don't just desire this role. They need it." [8]

Taking this description of marriage and applying it as an analogy to the church, we learn that only if we care about the church and the people in it will it be possible for us to be in conflict. In other words, conflict is a function of caring. It does seem that if someone is in conflict with us, he does not care about us, but the exact opposite is true. Where our relationships are tenuous, it will be highly unlikely that we will care enough to do battle with one another.

Bach says that intimacy requires all kinds of testing to get this evidence and it comes in many forms, one of which is conflict. Indeed the very existence of conflict may be a sign of deepening intimacy, for "it is when neither love nor hate can move a partner that a relationship is deteriorating." [9]

The elimination of the personal motives from conflict tends to lead toward sharper conflict. This is a difficult assumption to understand. It seems to fly in the face of many of our myths and presuppositions about Christian charity and the denial of self-interest. What this proposition asserts is that when you are in touch with what your motives are, you will tend not to idealize or dehumanize the battle; you will be less likely to carry it on as if it were a crusade for the *true, right, and just*. Lewis Coser in his book on social conflict writes: "Conflicts in which the participants feel that they are merely the representatives of collectivities and groups, fighting not for self but only for the ideals of the groups they represent, are likely to be more radical and merciless than those that are fought for personal reasons. Elimination of the personal element tends to make conflict sharper in the absence of modifying elements which personal factors would normally introduce." [10]

We have seen this illustrated many times. When a group is engaged in a conflict in the church, the group often sees the conflict merely in terms of the Children of Light (themselves) opposing the Children of Darkness (the others). The escalation from substantive issues to interpersonal categories is immediate and rapid. When it is not oneself for whom one is doing battle it is so easy to see the other as totally wrong and representative of evil, especially when one sees himself as a representative of good. When, on the other hand, one is searching his own motives, and is aware that some of his personal likes, dislikes, and needs are shaping his behavior, he will tend to temper his demands. Recognizing that his motives are not perfect, he will be less likely self-righteously to escalate his side of the conflict out of proportion to the substantive issues.

Conflict is less sharp in those groups which appeal to the periphery of one's personality. Again Coser says: "In groups in which relations are functionally specific and affectively neutral, conflicts are apt to be less sharp and violent than in groups wherein ties are diffuse and affective, engaging the total personality of their members. In effect, this suggests that conflicts in groups such as Rotary Clubs or Chambers of Commerce are likely to be less violent than in groups such as religious sects or radical parties. . . . Organizations of the latter kind aim at encompassing the total personality, hence the bond between the members is much stronger there than in groups where segmental types of relations prevail." [11]

This assumption is clearly understood by most ministers, who are aware that people's love and concern for the church is shaped not only by their commitment to the institution's goals but also by their relationship to the pastor as counselor, by experiences in the church that are personally significant to them, related to marriage, birth, and death, and by demands that are made on members to show their Christian commitment in all aspects of their lives. When conflict arises in the church, then, we are not talking about a conflict in an area of one's life where he is only segmentally involved. On the contrary, we are talking about a conflict in which a very large portion of one's total person is committed. Thus, one's resistance to change will be greater, and the degree of his concern for the outcome of the conflict will be greater as well.

The larger the number of conflicts, the greater the stability of the organization. Here is another of those assumptions which seem to go against logic and common sense. However, behavioral scientists [12] have been able to show that where there are only a few conflicts in an organization—and especially where there is only one —the organization tends to become more and more polarized. That is, every important decision to be made tends to be made only in relation to the major conflict. When a number of conflicts are operative simultaneously in the organization, groups tend to be formed from different personnel around different issues. Thus, in a local church, if all conflict is based on whether one is for the pastor or against him, there will tend to be heavy polarization. On the other hand, if several conflicts are going on simultaneously, it is more likely that factions will overlap, so that while an individual may be opposed to Mr. Jones on the new building issue, he may stand with Jones on the issue of trying new forms of worship. This means that it is difficult to place Jones in the category of the Children of Darkness, since he is an ally on some issues though an opponent on others. An organization that has these crosscurrents of conflict, then, is better able to manage the conflicts that arise, and is more stable. That organization which has only one or two conflicts will tend to polarize more heavily and be more likely to split into two or more parts.

The closer the group personally, the greater the threat the conflict poses. When conflict does occur in close groups it tends to be more threatening because people care more about one another and the effect of the other's response will be more deeply felt. When people begin to care more about each other, the amount of pain associated with the conflict will be much greater. Thus, closer groups tend to have more painful and sharper conflict because of the probability that more than just the issues will be at stake; interpersonal relationship and the fear of losing that relationship will also be at issue.

Where groups tend to suppress conflict, there will be an accumulation of feeling, leading toward a potentially dangerous conflict. A group in conflict can be like a pressure cooker: as the heat (conflict) increases, the pressure builds up. The more pressure, the greater the explosion if the pressure is not abated. Without continuous releases as a church moves along through its routine and small conflicts, pressure can build up causing a large explosion over a rather minor conflict. When this situation occurs, it puts the church in the rather embarrassing position of having to mobilize great energy and resources to deal with a rather insignificant problem. To people on the oustide the conflict seems petty and small. For example, we encountered a conflict where a minister lost his church over the question whether the memorial plaque for the church's members who have died would be in the narthex or in the social hall.

The problem is that there is a big assumption inscribed in the folklore of the church that anger, hostile feelings, conflict, and differences of opinion are signs of sickness, selfishness, and failure in a church. This assumption dictates hiding, suppressing, avoiding, and/or denying even the slightest twinge of dissatisfaction that one may have, because if he reveals it, he will disclose the fact that the church is not the strong superchurch it has been trying to make itself believe it is. Religiously believing this assumption, of course, means that people keep their emotions bottled up, and when the feelings finally emerge they are distorted and are usually expressed inappropriately. Thus, we are saying that conflict properly managed is conflict continually managed. The appropriate handling of conflict is helping people to express their feelings and deal regularly with the conflicts that are present. In this way, people's conflict management "muscle" does not atrophy but is continually exercised and used. Then, when it arises, conflict (either large or small) does not pose an immobilizing threat.

Notes

1. *The Dimensions of Human Conflict*, comp. by Ross Stagner (Wayne State University Press, 1967), p. 136.

2. Warren Schmidt and Robert Tannenbaum, "The Management of Differences," in Robert Tannenbaum, Irving Weschler, and Fred Massarik, *Leadership and Organ-*

ization (McGraw-Hill Book Co., Inc., 1961), pp. 101–118.

3. For a detailed discussion of these points, see Lewis Coser, *The Functions of Social Conflict* (The Free Press, 1956).

4. Richard Walton, *Interpersonal Peace Making, Confrontations and Third Party Consultation* (Addison-Wesley Publishing Company, Inc., 1969), p. 111.

5. *Ibid.,* p. 112.

6. See Robert Lee and Russell Galloway, *The Schizophrenic Church* (The Westminster Press, 1969), for a description of what happens to churches with a history of effective conflict management and what happens to those with little or none.

7. Walton, *op. cit.,* p. 112.

8. George Bach, *The Intimate Enemy: How to Fight Fair in Love and Marriage* (William Morrow & Company, Inc., 1969), p. 207.

9. *Ibid.,* p. 14.

10. Coser, *op. cit.,* p. 118.

11. *Ibid.,* pp. 68–69.

12. *Ibid., passim.*

3

Where to Begin

"Where to begin" is one of the hardest decisions con-fronting a person who senses trouble in the church. Does he go to a board meeting and "spill the beans"? Does he call a meeting of his friends to discuss the impending or present problem? Does he go to his bishop or denom-inational executive to describe his church's problems and difficulties?

We have seen churches successfully start at each of these points. In some cases the denominational exec-utive has been contacted and he has initiated conversa-tions with the proper boards of that church. In other cases attention has been called to the conflict through the pastor, official boards, or self-appointed committees. It really is not so important where the initiation of the concern develops. What is important is that the issues come to the surface and that they become the legitimate, open concern of everyone in the church.

Once there is sufficient awareness of the problem, then the problem can be managed. Without an open recognition of the problem—whether it is an official

recognition, i.e., a part of a board agenda, or an unoffi-
cial recognition where the aggrieved parties meet at
someone's home—it will not be possible to manage the
conflict. Therefore, in order to deal with the conflict, it
will be necessary to have some kind of initial meeting to
determine the extent of the problem as best as is possible
under the circumstances and to determine what kind of
response is called for in the church.

At this "surfacing meeting" one should try to have
persons present who represent the various sides of the
conflict; the group should try to determine what the
issues seem to be, who is in which camp, whether the
conflict is worth surfacing and working through, and
whether a referee should be called in. As will be described in a later chapter, a referee does not necessarily
have to be an outsider, but he or she must certainly not
be an advocate of the position held by any of the camps
that are involved in the conflict. A successful referee can
only be one who is outside the conflict, or what some
persons call a "third party."

It might be helpful at this initial meeting to share
Chart I with the persons present. This will give them a
picture of the options open to them and will make it
possible for them to go about decision-making in an
orderly way. In a conflict situation it is particularly difficult for persons to look seriously at the options they
have before them, and an examination of this chart
might help the group to understand some of the options
open to them.

The reader may find this chart helpful also as a guide
through this book since the chart is intended to serve
as an outline of the decision-making that a referee will
go through as he attempts to guide the conflict process.

Chart I. OPTIONS IN CONFLICT MANAGEMENT

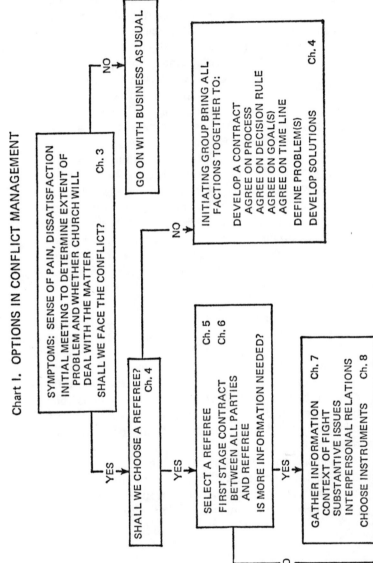

SYMPTOMS: SENSE OF PAIN, DISSATISFACTION
INITIAL MEETING TO DETERMINE EXTENT OF PROBLEM AND WHETHER CHURCH WILL DEAL WITH THE MATTER   Ch. 3

SHALL WE FACE THE CONFLICT?

NO → GO ON WITH BUSINESS AS USUAL

YES

SHALL WE CHOOSE A REFEREE?   Ch. 4

NO → INITIATING GROUP BRING ALL FACTIONS TOGETHER TO:

DEVELOP A CONTRACT
AGREE ON PROCESS
AGREE ON DECISION RULE
AGREE ON GOAL(S)
AGREE ON TIME LINE

DEFINE PROBLEM(S)
DEVELOP SOLUTIONS   Ch. 4

YES

SELECT A REFEREE   Ch. 5
FIRST STAGE CONTRACT BETWEEN ALL PARTIES AND REFEREE   Ch. 6

IS MORE INFORMATION NEEDED?

YES

GATHER INFORMATION   Ch. 7
CONTEXT OF FIGHT
SUBSTANTIVE ISSUES
INTERPERSONAL RELATIONS
CHOOSE INSTRUMENTS   Ch. 8

NO

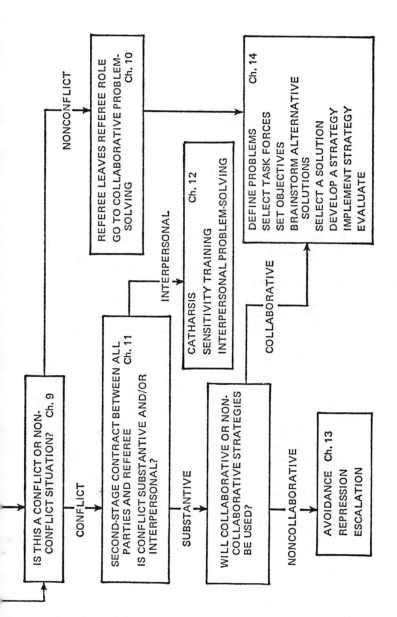

IS THIS A CONFLICT OR NON-CONFLICT SITUATION?   Ch. 9

NONCONFLICT

CONFLICT

REFEREE LEAVES REFEREE ROLE
GO TO COLLABORATIVE PROBLEM-SOLVING
Ch. 10

SECOND-STAGE CONTRACT BETWEEN ALL PARTIES AND REFEREE   Ch. 11
IS CONFLICT SUBSTANTIVE AND/OR INTERPERSONAL?

INTERPERSONAL

Ch. 12
CATHARSIS
SENSITIVITY TRAINING
INTERPERSONAL PROBLEM-SOLVING

SUBSTANTIVE

WILL COLLABORATIVE OR NON-COLLABORATIVE STRATEGIES BE USED?

COLLABORATIVE

NONCOLLABORATIVE

AVOIDANCE   Ch. 13
REPRESSION
ESCALATION

DEFINE PROBLEMS   Ch. 14
SELECT TASK FORCES
SET OBJECTIVES
BRAINSTORM ALTERNATIVE SOLUTIONS
SELECT A SOLUTION
DEVELOP A STRATEGY
IMPLEMENT STRATEGY
EVALUATE

4

Conflict Management
Without a Referee

If, after considering all the options open to it and carefully examining the costs and benefits of going ahead
with "surfacing" the conflict, the group decides that it
does not need to continue a conflict management process, it should decide to go on with business as usual.
This is a perfectly acceptable decision. On the one hand,
if the church continues to have the conflict and the
conflict gets worse, the decision, of course, can be recon-
sidered. On the other hand, if the conflict does not get
worse but disappears and there are still some (but only
a few) who think that something should be done, those
who considered the matter in the first place can relay
the thinking of the group and will be able to give well-
considered reasons for not taking action at that time.

If, however, the group decides that something must
be done, its next task is to determine whether a referee
should be used. It is the thesis of this book that in most
cases the use of a referee will lead to the best and longest-
lasting results of conflict management, and the substance

of the book is devoted to management strategies that assume the presence of a disinterested third party. It is quite possible that the group or the church may wish to manage the conflict without resorting to the use of this third party. In such a situation we would recommend the following course of action.

CONTRACTING TO MANAGE THE CONFLICT

In any conflict management situation that is not pure manipulation all parties that are or will be affected by the substance of the conflict must be involved in the management of the conflict. Therefore, nonrefereed conflict should begin by bringing all factions and parties together. In most cases this is best done on a Saturday or on another day when the affected persons will have the whole day to work through the various phases of the problem. The day-long meeting has several advantages. People start fresh and are not worn out from a hard day at work. There is time to work issues through, and there is also time for short breaks so the participants can catch their breath, but the breaks are not so long that persons will work themselves into an anxious defensiveness wondering what will be happening next.

Once all the parties who are affected by the conflict are in the same room, the group should attempt to develop a contract or covenant as to how they intend to work together to manage the conflict. In most covenants that we develop we like to write the "contract" informally on a piece of newsprint with a felt-tip pen or a crayon. The elements usually include the process that the group will go through, the decision rule that will be used, the group's goals, and a time by which it intends to accomplish its goals.

Agree on Process

When we are talking about the process, we are referring to those things which we might do together to manage the conflict, and we might agree on both what we will try to do and what we will try not to do. Thus a group may have written on their newsprint under "Process":

We will begin by giving both sides an opportunity to present their "case" fully.

Next there will be a special listening time to make sure that each side understands the other's point of view.

Then we will vote on recommended plans of action.

There will be no filibustering.

We will stick to the specific issues of the conflict.

The reader will note that there is a mixture of process and policy in this list, so that the list not only describes the methods the group will use but also qualifies the ways these methods will be used.

Agree on Decision Rule

With regard to the decision rule, this is a good issue to resolve before the time comes to make a decision related to the conflict. Some groups like to work strictly by consensus, which we consider to be an excellent though very slow process. Those groups which make decisions by bargaining ("We won't stop pledging if you will stop playing the guitar") or by hierarchy (very common in the Roman Catholic Church, where the pastor of a congregation has final authority) don't usually make decisions that last very long or decisions to which people are seriously committed. Voting, however, is usually a rather efficient compromise between the lengthy processes of consensus and the uncommitted results of hierarchy and bargaining. We have found it best not to assume that there is any special magic, however, in a majority vote. Especially in voluntary organizations where a 50–50 split can be devastating to future organizational life, one might want to consider 70 percent, or even 80 percent, to be the necessary number of votes before a resolution is considered adopted.

Agree on Goals

It is to be hoped that, in setting the goals in the contracting process, all parties to the conflict can become aware that their opponents and they have some common commitment to the church and its continuing health. It is so easy to see one's opponent as disinterested in the church or, worse yet, positively determined to destroy it. The goal-setting process can help all parties see that there is some real basis for consensus even though there are large areas of disagreement. Some goals that we have written on newsprint at this stage have been:

> Develop a church where we all feel like brothers and sisters in Christ.
>
> Develop a feeling of Christian unity.
>
> Help the church to be a place where we can manage our conflicts creatively.
>
> Get genuine understanding of one another's point of view.

As the parties to the conflict are putting these goals on paper and are agreeing on them, they are taking an important first step toward managing their difficulties. They are practicing collaborating and agreeing with one another, a very positive first step in conflict management.

Agree on Time Line

Finally, the group should agree on the time (hour or day) when work on this issue should be finished. Parkinson's law, stating that work expands to fill the time allotted to complete the task, is especially true in conflict. Indeed, it usually never enters a person's mind that he might set a time by which he will try to finish being in a fight, and therefore the fight never ends. Setting a time also gives the combatants less of a sense of continuing pain. In seeing a possible end to the conflict, they may be more inclined to work through their differences rather than to avoid and repress them.

After the contract has been agreed upon by all parties, the group should find some means to state exactly what the problems are that it is trying to solve. This is a most crucial phase of the management process. Here we would recommend that the reader pay careful attention to the material in Chapter 14 in the section "Make a Concrete Problem Statement."

Once the problems have been defined, then, through the use of the processes and decision rules determined in the contract phase, the group can determine what its strategies to solve its problems will be. If the group can get to this phase through the contract and problem definition phases, it should be able to work its difficulties through from here on without a referee. The earlier phases should have helped the group move from the feeling of fight to the feeling of problem-solving, and the fact that antagonists found themselves collaborating on process and goals will mean they will be more likely to find themselves collaborating on solutions to the issues that originally caused the conflict. If the group is not able to do this, it may be necessary to go back to the decision as to whether a referee should be called in.

5

The Referee

We searched for a clear image of the leadership that can move an impacted, stymied, polarized congregation through a fight and on to a constructive new level of organizational health. In the legal system, when a contest reaches an unresolvable impasse, the issue is put before a judge or a jury who hears and awards a decision. In labor negotiations, when bargaining has reached an impasse the services of a mediator are often utilized. The mediator assists each side to state its case clearly and suggests areas of agreement and disagreement along with options toward a resolution of the differences. The mediator attempts to bring the two sides to a point of common agreement without coercion. In real estate transactions an escrow agent acts as a third party holding the elements being exchanged (the property title and the funds) until all parts of the agreement have been met. In sports contests there are umpires, timekeepers, and linesmen, who function to keep the contestants within previously agreed upon rules for the contest. Each of these images provides some regulation of the contest, but each is inadequate to convey the full meaning of the role of the third party in a church fight.

The function of the judge in giving form and shape to the contest is crucial to this third-party role as we see it, but the function of awarding decisions is not useful in most church contexts. There have been church fights that have been decided by a higher authority, when denominational executives step in, but most often this means that the contestants have been unable to manage their own struggle. One church fight ended in the exodus of one part of the congregation when the church development division of the national office stepped in. Because this office held the mortgage to the property, it felt it had to enter the fight to protect its own interest, which was to maintain a congregation adequate to meet the mortgage payment responsibility.

The function of the labor arbitrator is instructive, for our purposes, in relation to the task of giving process to the contest and by acting as a third party to add new energy and optimism toward a resolution. An arbitrator is different from a mediator in that once both parties agree to submit the dispute to arbitration, the arbitrator's decision becomes binding, morally if not legally. The word "arbitrator" is also inadequate because of the implication that he has the power to decide who will be the winner or the loser.

Other words that are more management-oriented and that might be employed to clarify the leadership role appropriate to church fights are "conflict manager," "facilitator," "enabler," "conductor," "controller," "director." None of these is entirely satisfactory in our view. Words such as "conductor," "controller," and "director" have manipulative connotations in some settings and imply a hierarchical relationship that is not appropriate in volunteer organizations. Words such as "enabler" and "facilitator," however, are too weak and do not bring to mind the need for strong, confident leadership that is often called for in conflict situations.

The referee in a football or basketball game is much closer to the kind of role we wish to describe here. The referee directs the interchange between the contestants within the previously agreed upon rules for the game. He has the power to penalize parties who disregard the rules and he facilitates the process whereby each team can develop its strategy to accomplish its goals.

We prefer the designation "referee" because it does not have the connotation of declaring a winner and keeps before us the notion of neutrality, which is so crucial to the third-party role in conflict management.

Specifically, what we have in mind is that when contestants or advocates are engaged in a conflict, a third force is often critical to enable the conflict to be energizing, constructive, and useful rather than the debilitating, tearing, and wound-inflicting experience it so often is. What is needed is the development of internal resources within local congregations which can function as a neutral force when conflicts arise.

In Appendix I we have suggested external resources that can be called in to provide conflict management leadership, but this can be expensive. We have found that most congregations have resources—e.g., skillful and sensitive persons—who can, with practice, become very useful to that congregation in managing its conflicts. These are not always the same persons, but usually individuals can be found, for specific issues, who are neither protagonist nor antagonist and can function as referees.

THE EMERGENCE OF LEADERSHIP IN CONFLICT SITUATIONS

One obvious kind of leadership at work in conflict situations is given by those who lead the various factions or parties. We call these leaders "advocates." They have specific points of view on the issues under question and seek to gain support for their position. The other leadership upon which we are focusing is given by those who function to organize the process—the way in which the issues are confronted, negotiated, and decided. We call these leaders the "referees" in order to emphasize the third-force character of their role.

There are several constituencies in a local church out of which there may emerge one or more referees.

The Formal Leaders

Every church has formal leadership. These roles are filled by persons usually elected at the annual meeting. They are given authority by virtue of their election to these offices, which are normally listed in the bylaws. The formal leader who wants to function as a referee has the advantage of being able to call official meetings and set agendas. In addition, he has the normal influence that accrues to officeholders. One of the disadvantages is that he is often from the ranks of advocates on various crucial issues, is perceived by others to be an advocate, or has a history of deep involvement in whatever issue is in conflict. Thus, he may have allies and enemies already established, making refereeing difficult, if not impossible.

The Informal Leaders

Often some of the most powerful persons in a church do not hold formal office but are crucial to important decisions. Their power is in their use of influence, and they are often consulted by the people in authority (formal leaders) before important decisions are made. The basis of this influence is often that a person has been in the church a long time, has held office, has special expertise or experience, or has made large financial contributions to the church. The informal leader has the advantage of not being in power and is therefore not necessarily a defender of the current administration's point of view. But, here again, he can be perceived as nonneutral through past involvement in issues, giving him the same disadvantage as the formal leaders.

Inactive or Unknown Potential Leaders

We have found that most congregations often have inactive or marginally active lay people who have the resources to be a referee but have not been utilized. The unknown potential leader with skill would seem to have the advantage of potential trust from all sides among the advocates (although trust must be won). The advantage is a clean slate with few or no debts or credits on the record.

Smaller congregations are less likely to have such persons with both the skill and the clean slate. People tend to know each other well and to have had multilevel experience over a period of time. However, an adequate referee is someone not committed to any of the sides involved in the particular conflict for which resolution is being sought. With clarity as to one's role (both on the part of the referee and of the other participants), anyone can successfully perform this function.

QUALIFICATIONS FOR THE REFEREE

Here are some of the qualifications for a person in the referee role:

He doesn't take substantive conflict personally. In open, unrepressed conflict situations feelings run high, and negative feelings are directed at everyone, even at persons who perceive themselves to be helpers. Sometimes anyone who is involved in the conflict is perceived (by those who think conflict in itself is wrong) to be a part of the problem—even the third-party helper. The referee needs to have enough ego strength to help the parties join the substantive issues and yet not be overcome by the high emotions. In other words, difference, dislike, or disapproval do not immobilize him.

He has a high tolerance for ambiguity, ambivalence, and frustration. In most churches, healthy conflict processes have not been established, so that moving through conflict puts people into an unfamiliar and risky experience. This creates ambiguity and ambivalence at the feeling level. Because emotion runs high and the conflict itself has generated a high degree of commitment to one side or the other, moving toward resolution is slow, complex, and therefore frustrating. A person who cannot work in these conditions soon becomes tired and unresourceful at best; blocking and fear-producing at worst.

He is confident in conflict management and refereeing. Persons who are uncertain of themselves and cautious about their abilities to be helpful will communicate their fears to others, which will tend to move all parties to even more defensive positions. The single most helpful dimension of experience is to have the confidence that conflict can be resolved and that new, healthy organizational life and interpersonal relations await the completion of the process. Many persons already have this confidence and can be quite effective in the role of referee.

He is not an advocate for any particular solution, nor does he take sides on the issues in this conflict. This means that he will not be an advocate on this issue in this situation. Thus, in today's fight he is in a position to be a referee. In tomorrow's fight the same person might be defined as advocate and thus will not be qualified as a referee. This can be helpful for those situations in which a totally neutral resource on all issues cannot be found within the congregation and the church is mature enough to recognize and use a resource person who can change roles.

We have functioned as trainers and as organizers for social change, but we have been able to function as a referee in specific local churches because we have chosen to stay within the referee role and not push for those points of view for which, in other situations, we would be advocates. There have been times when the tension between the referee role and the advocacy role have become too great and we have had to share our dilemma with the group and move out of the referee role. We found that this is an irreversible change and in such cases a new referee must be found.

He is credible to both (all) sides. If all sides of the conflict do not find the referee credible, some will resist entering into the effort to find resolution to the conflict. This is another way of saying that each faction must see the referee as facilitating its self-interest before the referee can function usefully. Usually all sides fear losing the battle. They will be suspicious and will have little trust of the referee or the process if the fear is not overcome.

The referee is able to express strong feelings and to accept them in return. Our view of a healthy organization and healthy interpersonal relationships requires that feeling not be repressed but be expressed openly. The referee needs to model this behavior and help those for whom this is new behavior. Our conflict resolution process includes confronting and being honest at the interpersonal level. It requires a referee who is able not only to deal with the substance of the issues but to recognize that feelings are also strongly affecting behavior and commitment to issues. Feelings must, therefore, be dealt with just as profoundly as the issues.

The Referee's Assumptions

The referee's assumptions about conflict will shape the way he works and will affect the outcome of the fight. These are the expectations about conflict and refereeing which we have found to be helpful to referees.

Conflict is inevitable and resolvable. For the purposes

of contrast and clarification, let us compare several combinations of expectations or assumptions as to the inevitability and the resolvability of conflict. There are those who say that in group life conflict is not inevitable. These people usually operate on the norm that conflict is the sign of a breakdown of healthy organizational functioning, that conflict is a sign of failure. We contend that conflict is both inevitable in healthy organizational life and is a sign that people care about the organization and are investing themselves in its life.

There are those also who would contend that conflict is not resolvable, that human differences are so great that conflict is to be avoided at all costs. In this view, if conflict is not repressed, organizational life will disintegrate. Often, given this assumption, strong, controlling leadership emerges. We contend that conflict is resolvable, and therefore one can be optimistic about resolution when the conflict is dealt with. This does not mean resolution by finding the lowest common denominator. Rather, conflict properly managed can be the impetus for discovering new possibilities. For example, in one church considerable polarization had developed regarding whether to infuse the Sunday morning worship with contemporary music, dialogue sermons, and banners. The resolution that was developed and enthusiastically agreed upon by both the advocates of traditional worship and the advocates of contemporary worship was to establish a separate, evening service entirely devoted to contemporary worship expression. Both sets of advocates were able to worship as they desired and could take pride in the multidimensional ministry of their church.

Conformity is not required. Being caught or trapped within the culture (the operating values or the usual patterns of reacting) of an organization hinders creative processes for reconciliation. To improve a social system, the referee must be able to step out of the culture and yet be sensitive to what is happening in it (while not becoming alienated from it). This is what gives a referee perspective on the situation. Some typical cultural dynamics that reveal operational values not helpful to conflict management in churches are: avoidance and repression of differences, talking about problems only on the telephone to your grapevine, referring all decisions to the minister, etc. Recognizing these dynamics and naming them helps people to see how they are operating and to choose new modes of working together. The referee's assumption is that he can serve a useful purpose by facilitating the process as an "outsider," that is, one who stands outside, or apart from, this conflict.

Few situations are hopeless. If the referee has optimism regarding the chances for meaningful organizational change, he increases his psychological freedom and that of others who are trying to move through a conflict situation. There is tremendous evidence from the behavioral sciences that profound changes can occur in the behavior of individuals and organizations. Few situations are hopeless. Making this assumption and operating in the spirit of hopefulness frees the individual or group to generate new possibilities in what might seem to others to be a hopeless situation.

One part affects another. Taking a systems approach also provides psychological freedom. By this we mean looking at the total organization as a system of interrelated parts and taking cognizance of the fact that changes in one subpart of the system will affect other parts.

For example, in a church that was highly polarized over three major issues, one of which was the expenditure of benevolence monies, the newly appointed minister took only the benevolence conflict as the focus for management in his first year. A satisfactory resolution in this area was worked out, and a new feeling of success was experienced which significantly changed the church's style in facing the other two issues. Optimism, confidence, and new energy created by this success helped significantly as the church approached each of the other conflicted issues. As a result, resolutions for them were easily found.

Each side probably has a piece of the truth. Attempting to see the conflict from the point of view of each advocate can help facilitate meaningful and helpful exchange. The referee can help the parties on all sides of the conflict to gain increased clarity about the views of each side. Polarization tends to create extreme interpretations and distorted projections about how the other side thinks and feels. The resolution process will be moved ahead if the referee helps generate clearer "real" pictures on all sides of the dispute.

There is some similarity between opponents. Closely related to the assumption that there is some validity in the other's point of view is attempting to find in oneself the shortcomings he perceives in the other.

Anatol Rapoport calls this the assumption of similarity:

> The most promising way to induce the assumption of similarity is to make it oneself. In common invective-evoking debates, one usually projects one's own shortcomings, aggressive urges, etc., on the other. What is pro-

posed here is the reversal of this procedure: one seeks within oneself the clearly perceived shortcomings of the opponent. The opponent often seems stupid or rigid or dishonest or ruthless. It will serve us well to ask ourselves to what extent we resemble him. This is recommended not on moral grounds but as a measure to insure a greater success in our effort. To convince, we must be heard, and to be heard, we must be listened to; people listen most attentively to what they like to hear; they like to hear their own shortcomings projected on others, not others' shortcomings projected on them. Our ultimate purpose in raising questions about ourselves is to induce the opponent to raise similar questions about himself. We see ourselves as intelligent, honest, and considerate. It will often serve us well to imagine that the opponent possesses these qualities to *some* degree. Maybe he does not, but maybe this "delusion" of ours will induce a similar delusion in him about us. I am, of course, discussing the psychological set conducive to conflict resolution. There is no question that such a set is necessary and often sufficient for resolving conflicts in a great variety of interpersonal and social situations.[1]

Present problems are the ones to solve. It is important to deal with the here and now, to start with what is *now* going on in the organization. There is often the tendency either to rehash old battles and hurts from a past history that cannot be changed or to work on fantasized futures that are unlikely to occur. The referee's task is to help the church learn to deal with problems and conflicts as they emerge, concentrating on the here and now. Except when venting is required, the "I remember . . . " issues are not helpful. And it is generally not helpful to deal with the "What if . . . " issues. Since our view is that in a lively church conflicts will inevitably emerge, the referee's objective is not to try to create an organization that has no problems. Such an organization would be a very dumb, shallow, and depressing kind of place. The referee's objective is to help develop a conflict resolution process that will be useful as the life of the organization is now developing, and this is most effectively done by working on real conflicts currently experienced in the church, not on remembrances and dreams.

The process is of great importance. This leads to another, closely allied assumption. There is a distinction between *content*, the various points of view, and the *process*, the pattern of exchange and the rules or norms governing the ways in which the views are brought into relationship. The content is *what* is worked on. The process is *how* the work is done. The advocate's concern is primarily about the content, the views he holds on the issues at hand. The referee is more focused in his work on the process, the way in which the work is carried out.

There is no right answer. The referee should be conscious that there are always a variety of processes for working on problems. There is no single right way or process. Often this assumption can provide psychological freedom and help the referee to move a church away from stereotyped or programmed behavior. Even suggesting a new process helps a group to expand the possibilities before it. Recognizing these choices and making decisions about them will assist the referee in unlocking polarized energy.

The Minister as Referee

Many ministers perceive their function in the church as *reconciler of differences* rather than as advocate for a specific point of view. This is especially true for those churches patterning themselves after the pluralistic model described in Chapter 1. A special word needs to be said about this in conflict situations.

Let us get at the issue by stating two conflicting truisms, both of which are illuminating for the minister considering the referee role in his own church:

Everyone wants to be the savior in tough situations.

Nobody likes a go-between.

With regard to the first, there is great appeal in remaining above the battle, in keeping one's hands clean, and then, in strategically intervening in the struggle with just the right word or insight to set the ship straight again. Then, one may be hailed as a hero for his resourcefulness. This is *not* what we mean by being a referee: this is a magician or manipulator. It assumes that the minister knows what is best for others (a highly dubious assumption), that a minister can provide what is best (also doubtful), and that his actions will be perceived by all to be helpful (ridiculous).

Our experience is that most ministers who have been working in a church for a time cannot function in the referee role even if the concept of reconciliation has been the primary focus for their ministry. Three reasons have led us to this conclusion:

First, most ministers perceive reconciliation as leading to a peaceful church which is distinguished by the absence of conflict. What is really going on in this situation is the repression of conflict for the sake of peace. This may be called reconciliation, but it is only a cease-fire.

Second, most ministers, by virtue of their formal leadership, have taken a position by word or deed on most issues. Therefore, a minister cannot be and will not be perceived as a trustworthy referee by all sides.

Third, most ministers are surprised to learn that some parties in the conflict perceive them to be a part of the problem rather than the solution. In one case, the minister's self-perception was that he had maintained a neutral position on an important issue but he discovered that both sides in the conflict perceived him as adverse to their cause ("If you're not with us, Mr. Leader, you're against us"). He thought that he could play the referee role, that he could be the reconciler he thought he was. However, after we entered the situation it took only a few data-gathering interviews to see that he was too deeply enmeshed in the problem to be the referee, even though he had tried to remain above the conflict.

With regard to the second truism, refereeing is a risky and thankless role to play. Among the risks are:

a. The referee will reach a conclusion about the "right" answer to the conflict. He then becomes an advocate for his own position and simply another party to the struggle. Most clergy have been trained to "come up with the answer." When he does not, he *is* refereeing, but is often perceived as abdicating his leadership role.

b. One who has high needs for inclusion and affection will feel very unsatisfied as a referee. This is because he cannot be a part of any group involved in the conflict, and he is likely to feel quite lonely.

c. The referee, as go-between, can easily become the common enemy of the contending advocates. This is often a transference of hostility onto what seems to be a safer target. Often, ministers get into trouble in this way. Our view is that the referee, in the final analysis, is not a go-between. The "going between" must be done by the advocates themselves with the referee's encouragement and assistance. He cannot do it for them.

THE DEVELOPMENT OF REFEREE SKILLS

For those who would be interested in further developing refereeing skills we would briefly indicate the three basic elements in the development process:

First, become familiar with the conceptual and research data on what happens to persons and groups in conflict (see Bibliography). We have drawn heavily on this material in this book.

Second, get as much experience as possible in group dynamics. Practice under the guidance of experienced persons.

Third, work at disciplined reflection with members of groups with whom you work and also with peers. Our rule is to work in teams of at least two referees. We give substantial time for reflecting on our experience, emphasizing the strengths and weaknesses of the design for processing the fight. We also carefully examine our individual behavior as perceived by the other members of the team.

Using Outside Resources

Although we have emphasized the identification, development, and utilization of internal resources for this referee role, there may be many situations that call for the use of outside resources. Some reasons for calling on outside resources are:

> The conflict is urgent and time is short.
>
> Everyone is either an advocate or has declared for one side or another.
>
> No one can be found in the church who will function as referee.
>
> The scale or complexity is beyond the range of resources available.
>
> There is no trust in internal resources.

In such situations, we would suggest four categories of resources outside the church:

Paid consultants. Schools of management at universities and colleges are very likely to have resources at a fee. It is important to get information about past work that they have done. (We have found that not all people who teach management can practice it.)

Resources from other churches. Often other churches can provide referee leadership. Again, it is crucial to get people who have been through the experience before and who know what they are doing.

Denominational resources. Some denominational offices at the national and regional level have people who specialize in refereeing conflict. Our experience is that many of these people are very skillful, whereas others have no skill at all (some are in the position by virtue of tenure rather than of competence). Denominational officers have the disadvantage of bringing bureaucratic self-interest into the local church and many want to force binding arbitration. Another disadvantage of denominational officers is that often they have considerable influence or power over the career of the local minister. This adds tension and inhibits their success as referees.

Ecumenical resources. In some areas, councils of churches or other bodies have established training and consulting resources. Often these are subsidized by denominational grants and are available at low or no cost. Further, they are clearly *for* the church they are working with and do not carry the self-interest or power disadvantages of denominational staff. Be sure to assess their credentials, however. Most ecumenical facilities with competent staff will be associated with the Action Training Coalition, The Association of Clinical Pastoral Educators, an accredited seminary, or the Association for Religion and Applied Behavioral Science.

NOTE

1. Anatol Rapoport, *Fights, Games, and Debates* (University of Michigan Press, 1960), pp. 306–307.

6

First-Stage Contract

Once the church has selected a referee to help manage its fight, the next task is for the referee and all parties affected by the conflict to develop a contract as to what information will be sought before there is an attempt to manage the conflict. The contracting with a referee should be in two stages.

The first stage ought to have to do with an agreement as to what information will be needed before the group can continue, what each person's role will be, and what policies or rules will be followed as to appropriate and inappropriate behavior. Thus, a church that is struggling with a conflict as to whether to use a denominational or nondenominational curriculum in the Sunday school may wish to clarify which persons are advocates and which persons are referees. In addition to this, the church certainly would want to decide what kind of information it needs to have in order to make a decision about the kind of material it will use: What constitutes appropriate pedagogical methodology? What kind of theological and Biblical content is fitting to the church?

How do people feel about each other personally in the context of the fight? and What experience has the church had with fights before? The group may also wish to make a list of appropriate and inappropriate behavior in the context of the conflicted decision-making. When persons from all sides are given a chance to contribute to such a list, there is usually consensus from all parties to a list similar to the following:

Each person should be honest about what he really thinks and feels.

Anything that gets said about the conflict outside regularly called meetings should be repeated in front of all participants.

Arguments must be specific and not generalized.

Name-calling is not helpful.

Each person will try to understand the others' points of view.

And so on.

After the first-stage contract is agreed upon, the group should decide whether it has enough information to skip the data-gathering phase. If it has, the group can go on to complete the second-stage contract. This second or management stage would include the items that were described in Chapter 4 on managing the conflict without a referee. That is, the group should agree on its process, decision rule, goals(s), and time line. However, it is usually the case that before the group can agree on these matters a good deal of information is needed.

Many leaders in the church come to a conflict situation with their minds already made up as to what is the cause of the trouble. Often there will be one or two who have ready platitudes to prove that they have the solution to all problems past, present, and future: "It all

starts with the individual," or "The trouble with the
clergy today is ——————," or "What we have to do is
change people's theology," etc. These statements have
assumptions at their root which conveniently locate and
define the problem in all situations. The trouble is that
each situation is different, and handy-dandy solutions
and analyses, though convenient for the pontificator,
are seldom relevant to the problem.

When a group is controlled by the individual or individuals who mouth these sayings, it stays trapped in the
very difficulties that caused the conflict. In order to cir-
cumvent this temptation to use old assumptions about
people and how they operate in organizations, it is of
paramount importance that the church seriously engage
in a carefully chosen process of gathering all information
relevant to the problem, analyzing the data, defining the
problem, and then looking at alternative strategies for
solutions. Therefore, we strongly suggest that after the
first-stage contract is made, the group should decide
what information it needs in order to choose a means
for carrying out the conflict management process.

7

Determining What
Information Is Needed

Three kinds of information are usually needed before
one can move ahead with the management process:
1. What issues and problems are being worked on?
2. How do people feel about each other as persons?
3. What is the context of the fight?
Answers to all three of the questions are necessary
before one can choose an appropriate method to manage the fight. The referee should therefore help the group
get clarity as to the questions it wants to ask and the way
it wants to get its information.

The reader should not find it difficult to think of questions that he or she would ask in any conflict as to the
substance of the confrontation. Usually the advocates
will be full of resources as to appropriate questions in
this area. It will also be rather easy to determine the
kind of information that one will need in order to understand how the various parties to the conflict feel about
each other.

Something that will probably be new to the reader,
however, is a consideration of the context in which the

fight is taking place. The rest of this chapter will focus
on areas related to the context of the fight on which the
referee and advocate might also want to gather information.

CONTEXT AREAS TO BE CONSIDERED

Extent of Polarization

One of the most difficult kinds of conflict situations
to manage is two-pole conflict where all the issues in the
church cut across the same constituency. This is the
case where individuals identify themselves with their
"camp," and make their decisions as to how they will
stand on each issue in relation to how their team stands.
This is what happens in two-party politics (if it really
works the way party leaders hope it will). "Good" party
members do not vote according to an issue's merit, but
in the way their party had decided that they should vote.
In a local church, this two-pole situation often can be
described as the liberals versus the conservatives. Instead
of deciding the issues of worship style, fund-raising
strategy, and fund dispersal on the basis of each issue's
merit, usually the parties stick together, decide their
policy beforehand, and vote as a bloc.

A more complex form of polarization occurs where
there are multiple parties rather than only two. Instead
of liberals versus conservatives there are many factions
that consistently vote as blocs within the church. For
example, in one church there were the following groups:
a religious ecstatic group (they controlled Wednesday
and Sunday night prayer meetings), a fundamentalist
group (they had the Sunday school), and a neo-orthodox

group (they controlled Sunday morning worship). Each group was homogeneous and only responded in defensive ways to the other groups.

The significant thing about polarization (whether it be two-pole or multi-pole) is that there are united constituencies. The unity of the party (and, incidentally, the maintenance of the conflict) is more important than responsible decision-making. Typical divisions in the church where conflict often gets manifested are: age (older versus younger); sex (women's groups versus "sexists"); race or ethnic origin (black versus white; those who wish to maintain the Old Country's tradition versus those who adapt to the ways of the New World); class (this often gets manifested in conflicts over how charismatic the worship service should be); ordination (lay versus clergy); office (church officers versus non-officers); and theology (those who believe it is the mission of the church to prepare individuals for the next world versus those who believe its mission it to prepare them to live in this world).

A third kind of polarization, and, in our opinion, by far the most healthy, occurs where the constituencies shift as the issues shift. Where, for example, there is a 50–50 split in a church on the issue of the kind of worship that will be held, Mr. Jones and Mr. Smith are in different camps. However, on the issue of whether there will be a coffeehouse for teen-agers in the social hall, the church may be split 70–30, with Mr. Smith and Mr. Jones in the same camp, and so on. In this situation, people experience each other as opponents on some issues and as allies on others. The constituencies shift as the issues shift—each person makes up his own mind on the basis of the issue rather than on the constituency of the factions. Conflict, here, is not experienced as threatening the basic consensus, but as a tool for sharpening and clarifying the issues and helping to get out as much information as possible.

Norms and Values

Other data relevant to the referee of a conflict situation are the norms and values in the church's culture related to conflict. Where there is a clear though unwritten norm that conflict is to be suppressed and avoided (and that when it emerges it is a sign of weakness or failure), this will have to be taken into account when one begins to develop strategies for managing the conflict. We have found that in many churches there is a great deal of resistance to working on the conflict because of this unwritten standard of behavior. It is then appropriate to do some training and education of the congregation in order to help people recognize that conflict is not necessarily a sign of failure, and may even be a sign of hope, before beginning to actually work on the conflict itself.

Past History

The church's history in dealing with conflict will weigh heavily on how it deals with it in the present. We recommend the book by Lee and Galloway, *The Schizophrenic Church.* One of Lee's major points from his study of the experience that six churches in northern California had with conflict is that having had good experience with conflict in the past and having worked out procedures for managing the conflict was very important for the successful congregational conflict-coping. However, he said, "the simple act of throwing them in the water will not ensure rapid improvement in swimming. Evidently there is more to it than mere quantity of exposure to conflict. This 'something more' has to do with the quality of the congregations' experience with conflict." [1] Thus, where the church has methods that have been used successfully in the past, they ought to be used in the present. If these successes are not there, new processes (which the congregation should see as experimental, or pilot, projects) ought to be tried.

Individual Capability

One must take into consideration the individual capability of each church member to handle conflict. Every situation is different, and in some churches it is very possible that a number of the members are quite fragile and insecure, whereas in other churches the leaders and membership are strong, self-confident, and experienced in dealing with substantive and interpersonal conflict. The choice of strategy will be strongly affected by the assessment of each member's ability to cope with conflict situations.

Amount of Time

We must consider the time we have to work in a given situation. Usually we have plenty of time. That is, most often we are not working under the conditions of an emergency or deadline, and the church can take the time it needs to work through its decisions. Occasionally the time is short, however, and the decisions must be made quickly in order to handle the situation. It is important in this kind of circumstance that a decision about how much time is available be based on the facts of the situation and not on the feelings of urgency that arise in the midst of a painful conflict situation.

Avoiding Explosion

Another consideration has to do with the ability of the organization and the individuals within it to avoid what Lee calls sheer, uncontrollable explosion. We have been in a number of situations where the participants did not feel it was inappropriate to abuse people or property. This kind of uncontrolled explosion takes the form of shouting matches where no communication is going on or where people verbally abuse one another and then storm out (of either the meeting or the church) in an angry display of temper. Thus, as one is preparing to develop a strategy to manage the conflict, he will have to take into account the realistic possibility of conflict getting out of control of those who wish to manage it.

Conflict's Cost

In every conflict situation valuable energy will be utilized in carrying on the conflict. Serious thought must be given, when deciding whether it is appropriate to escalate the conflict, as to what the probable consequences of any given action will be. If the conflict is faced at this time, will it mean that there will be a continuing, discomforting gnawing that is the undertone of most of what is done? If the conflict isn't dealt with, will it go away? If it is dealt with, will the church lose members? How many? How can this assumption be tested?

Ability to Stay on Issues

Another consideration has to do with one's capability to keep the discussion focused on real issues. Coleman [2] describes what often happens in conflict situations in churches as a progression from a single-issue difference to intense polarization. In his monograph on community conflict he describes this progression:

(1) Initial single issue.
(2) Disrupts equilibrium of community relations.
(3) Allows previously suppressed issues against opponent to appear.
(4) More and more of opponent's beliefs enter into the disagreement.
(5) The opponent appears totally bad.
(6) Charges against opponent as a person.
(7) Dispute becomes independent of initial disagreement.

With this kind of process possible and probable in heavy conflict situations, we must be keenly aware of (a) how far the conflict has progressed, (b) how far it is likely to progress if someone doesn't intervene, and (c) the ability of the combatants to recognize the extent to which the conflict is in control of them rather than they being in control of the conflict.

Relevance of Conflict to Goals

We must also be able to assess the relevance of the conflict to the church's goals. Some conflicts are very interesting, but totally irrelevant to the work of the organization. Helping the church to assess whether or

not this conflict is relevant to its life situation can be a
major consideration in deciding whether one wants to
try to repress or avoid the conflict rather than to try to
deal with it "up front" with the congregation or church
leadership. There will probably be some who will say
that all conflicts are relevant in God's eyes and that the
church must therefore be involved in every fight that
develops. This is not our view. We feel that conflicts
ought to be avoided or repressed when they have little
to do with individual, organizational, or social growth
and development.

Openness of Communication

It is important to know to what extent lines of communication are open between the contending parties.
At times the parties are not communicating at all with
each other, so that refereeing the conflict between them
is very difficult. At other times there are ample opportunities for communication, such as gatherings where
both sides are present, but even with much talk there is
little communication. Messages are being sent but they
are not being received (at least they are not received
with understanding).

Amount of Investment

One must assess the amount of investment that each
side has in the issue itself. The amount of hostility, the
amount of energy that one is willing to invest, the
amount of risk that one is willing to take, and the length
of time one will stay in the battle will depend heavily
on how important one feels the issue to be. We are not
talking about how important the referee thinks the issue
is, but how important the antagonists see the issue to be.

This also will affect the style and strategy one uses to manage the conflict.

Substantive or Interpersonal Conflict

The extent to which the conflict is substantive or interpersonal will also affect the choice of strategies one uses. Usually one will find a mixture of the two kinds of conflict, for where important issues are involved, significant feelings about persons will also be generated. We prefer to try to differentiate between what is substantive in the conflict and what has to do with personal feelings. This makes it possible to attempt first to work through the feelings so that we can then move on to issues of substance. Unless we deal with the feelings first, however, it will be nearly impossible for us to move on to deal with the substantive issues. Therefore, we will next discuss managing interpersonal conflict and then examine managing substantive conflict, recognizing that in most situations it may be necessary to be managing both kinds of conflict simultaneously.

Notes

1. Robert Lee and Russell Galloway, *The Schizophrenic Church* (The Westminster Press, 1969).

2. James S. Coleman, *Community Conflict* (The Free Press, 1957), p. 11.

3. *Ibid.*, p. 159.

8

Choosing a
Data-Gathering Instrument

Once the referee and the parties to the conflict have a general idea of what information is needed, they must determine how to gather that information. In this chapter we will be looking at various methods of obtaining relevant information from a church so that we can define the problem, establish our change goals, and go to work on accomplishing them. But before we look at these methods we should say a word as to what we are talking about when we discuss "facts" or "data" or "information." "Data" is anything that may have bearing on the state the church is in at the moment. Behavior (what people do and what they do not do to and with each other) is data. Feelings are data—what people feel affects very much the way they behave, and it is important to know what people's feelings are toward the church or a particular facet of it. The way the church is structured (both polity and building) is data. The church's polity affects the way people communicate with each other, and the church building not only symbolically describes what goes on within it but also affects commuication and the implementation of the church's strategies. Past experiences of the church and of the people within it are data, as are the theology of the church's members, the church's power structure, goals, communications processes, evaluation processes, financial situation, traditional uses of time and space, boundaries (who is a member and who is not), perpetuation processes, and so on. All these things are data that can be analyzed.

We use four methods for gathering information or data: questionnaires, interviews, small-group discussion, and direct observation. We will examine each method in turn, looking at the problems and values to be found in each method. We shall then make some suggestions for the best utilization of each method.

QUESTIONNAIRES

Of the many kinds of questionnaires, we use three most often: open-ended, scaled response, and multiple choice. The open-ended questionnaire is made up of sentence-completion statements, such as these:

The best sermons I have heard in the past four years in this church were on the subject of _____.

I think the greatest problem facing our church at this time is _____.

I think the worship service in our church could be improved by _____.

It is up to the respondent to develop his own categories of response and to the reader of the questionnaire to interpret what the response means. An effective questionnaire of this type must have questions and statements worded clearly enough so that most of the respondents will give answers that are meaningful to the reader. In other words, a statement such as, "I think the work of our church is _____," is not clear as to whether a response should be made with regard to the church's purpose, the way committee work is done, or the accomplishment of goals. Response to this statement would likely be difficult to interpret, especially if the respondents put only one word, such as "lousy" or "great."

Another type of questionnaire is the scaled response. This instrument has the following form:

I think the climate of trust in this church is:

1   2   3   4   5   6   7
(very low)   (real and expressed)

I think the minister's sermons are:

1   2   3   4   5   6   7
(poor)   (excellent)

After worship on Sunday, I feel:

1   2   3   4   5   6   7
(let down or angry)   (inspired and ready to act)

This kind of instrument is especially good for quantifying the results. After tallying the results of the questionnaires that are returned, one has a means of quantifying areas of greater or lesser concern. This kind of questionnaire is best used when the persons seeking the information have little knowledge of where the source of the conflict might be. By asking questions in many areas of the church's life, one may hit upon one or two areas that stand out in terms of significantly lower response. When tallying the score, be sure to indicate how many respondents designated each point on the scale. Averages don't tell much. So the completion statement, "I think the minister's sermons are:" should be scored as follows,

1	2	3	4	5	6	7
10	0	0	0	0	0	10

with twenty persons responding on both the extremely high and the lowest ends of the scale. An average for this scoring would indicate the church's response to be "4," which would not reveal the extreme polarization present in responses.

A third kind of questionnaire is the multiple choice. It looks like this:

I think the climate of trust in our church:
   ( ) is nonexistent
   ( ) exists only in certain cliques
   ( ) exists at all levels of church life

I think the minister's sermons are:
   ( ) poorly prepared
   ( ) well prepared
   ( ) poorly delivered
   ( ) well delivered
   ( ) abstruse
   ( ) to the point

The multiple choice questionnaire is as quantifiable as the scaled response, and it helps the responder along by reminding him of some categories of response he may not have remembered. For example, one may be highly critical of the minister's sermon delivery but quite happy with the content. A response to an open-ended question about the sermons might be "lousy," and unless there are a number of questions on sermon preparation, delivery, and content, the answers may not be clear. Some of these difficulties may be handled, then, by a multiple choice questionnaire. Of course, the biggest problem with this kind of instrument is that the questioner may have left out some vital areas, thus blocking the possibility of gathering certain data.

Some of the values of using questionnaires are:

The answers are rather easy to interpret.

The results are quantifiable.

It is a very fast method for gathering data from large groups.

There is wide acceptance of the method.

Anonymity may bring to light previously undisclosed sentiment.

Some of the problems with questionnaires are:

The questions may not be understood by the respondents.

The respondents may not believe that their responses will be taken seriously.

Different persons may give different meanings to the same questions.

It is easy not to respond to any of the alternatives.

Because of the impersonal form of a questionnaire, individuals who feel that they have concerns of a personal nature are not likely to share their concerns.

With regard to how questionnaires are best administered, we would make these recommendations: First, try to involve as large a portion of the conflicting parties as possible in designing the questionnaire and deciding how it will be distributed and evaluated. It is important to find areas where the conflicting parties can have an opportunity to collaborate and experience some success at working together. Developing a questionnaire can be a good opportunity for the "warring" factions to have an experience of each other that has the possibility of being successful collaboration. This kind of experience can help to de-escalate the conflict as each party sees the other as competent, human, resourceful, and able to work with others in a noncombatant role.

Second, make sure that all significant actors in all camps are involved in the design, implementation, and evaluation of the questionnaire's results. Otherwise the results will be written off as rigged and as not sensitive to those who were left out.

Third, it is highly imperative that the results of the survey be shared with all concerned and that these results be used to lead to real engagement with people. Many persons distrust questionnaires for the reason that after they have filled them out nothing happens. The results must be fed back to those who filled out the questionnaires, and those same people must then be immediately involved in a process of trying to figure out what to do with what they have learned.

Finally, we would recommend that the feedback of the data from the questionnaires (whether they were scaled, open-ended, or multiple choice) should be done (a) when there is plenty of time to deal with what has emerged (Sunday after church during the coffee hour is a poor time), (b) when all parties can be fully represented, and (c) within the structure of a previously agreed upon process for hearing the results of the data-gathering. After all the parties have heard the data, they can then determine what it means, what their specific problems are, and how they want to deal with

them. We recommend, at this stage, that the data be
shared and that the group establish what issues (problems) it sees as priority concerns. Then processes can be
established to deal with these issues.

INTERVIEWS

The interview process is really a form of the questionnaire. The difference is that each person has an opportunity to respond orally, rather than in writing, to questions about his church. The two major kinds of interviewing are the *directed interview* with open-ended questions (usually from an interview "schedule") and the
nondirective interview. In the directed interview the
interviewer or interviewers determine before they begin
which areas they would like to explore with the interviewee. Usually a schedule of questions is written out
that looks similar to an open-ended questionnaire.

The nondirective interview, however, does not use
such a schedule. The interviewer simply establishes con-
tact with the interviewee, makes him feel as much at
home as possible, and then says something like, "What
would you like to tell me about the church?" Or, I am
here to find out what your expectations and concerns
are about the church. Can you tell me what you think
about it?"

The values in using the interview process are:

　It lets the interviewer explore new areas of concern
　　that he may not have thought of when he was
　　developing a schedule or questionnaire.

　It facilitates private elaboration of the interviewee's
　　point of view. (Many find it hard to express

exactly what they feel, and conversation with another person helps them to say what they wish to say.)

A skilled interviewer can explore ideas and emotions that the interviewee may at first resist exploring.

A skilled interviewer can be aware of the relevance of certain data that are generated through other means of communications than the words themselves (such as intonation, "body language," showing up late or wanting to leave early).

The problems with interviewing are:

It takes a long time.

If the interviewer is not competent (or is seen as an enemy agent), he can make matters worse.

During the feedback phase the group is highly dependent on the interviewer's interpretation of the data, and there may even be some resistance developed just on this issue.

In the use of this method, we would encourage consideration of the following:

1. It is often helpful to begin the interview by assuring the interviewee that anything he says will be confidential with regard to the source but not as to the content. Thus, one might indicate that he will tell others what he has learned about the way various people in the church feel but that he will not reveal specifically who said what.

2. Feedback presented verbatim is going to have greater impact than feedback presented thematically. Thus, if one reports his findings thematically ("fifteen persons are unhappy about the organization of the minister's sermons"), he is going to generate less heat than if he reports verbatim ("The guy doesn't prepare," or

"Reverend Jones drives people out of the church with his wandering dissertations"). Verbatim feedback may be needed; we are pointing out that one must make a strategic decision as to which method is appropriate. The use of verbatim feedback is often helpful when there is much suppression and denial of the conflict. It helps to make the case for doing something about the situation.

3. Don't allow advocates who are clearly identified with one side or the other to be interviewers. If there are no individuals in the church who can be identified as neutral and a person insists on using this method, he should either hire an outside consultant or bring in denominational executives (or some people from a neighboring church) to be interviewers for the church.

4. Before the results of the interviewing are fed back to the congregation, all the key people should be informed about what will be shared. This would mean that if there are two factions in the church, with clearly identified leadership on each side, the interviewers should have a small meeting with (*a*) the key leaders of each faction, (*b*) the key leaders in the church if they are not the same, and (*c*) the pastor. This is a simple matter of keeping faith and building trust and confidence.

SMALL-GROUP DISCUSSION

Small-group discussion is our preferred way of gathering data in a local church. It's fast, it's immediate, the data are immediately verifiable, and one can work at several levels of conflict at once.

There are a number of ways to go about using this method. Some churches prefer to have small-group meetings in private homes, and the information from each of these groups is fed to appropriate committees or church plenary sessions. Other churches prefer to hold large meetings to which the entire membership is invited. The large group is then divided into small groups which caucus and give input to the larger groups. Still others prefer to have small-group meetings over a rather long period of time and to incorporate Bible study or theological reflection with their data-gathering processes. (However, we recommend that this method be used very carefully; it provides too accessible a cudgel for warring factions to do battle couched in the language of the gospel and hidden in platitudes as to how "*you* should love one another.")

Another thing one needs to consider in using this method is what instruments he will use to generate discussion. Actually, we do not believe that the choice of instruments here is a crucial one. Somehow churchmen usually find a way to say to each other what they have to say, no matter how cumbersome, slick, or pretty the instrument.

Nonetheless, here are a number of instruments we have used and have found effective:

Have the members of subgroups make composite collages or drawings of the church and share them with the rest of the group.

Have the group develop a small, scaled questionnaire to be filled out by each individual, and share the combined results of the questionnaires with the group for discussion and clarification.

Ask the group to talk about the subject(s) over

which the conflict has emerged in an open-ended interview fashion.

Have the group put itself physically into a kind of living "statue" or "machine" or diorama that represents how the church is now functioning. The members of the group can then discuss what they have learned about the church from the representation and how it was put together. This is not recommended for most churches because it may be quite threatening to some persons.

Have the group draw a time line of the significant events that have gotten the conflict to where it is now. Chart II is an abbreviated form of such a time line.

Chart II. TIME LINE

6/63	Rev. Mr. Jones arrives
6/64	Jones preaches sermon on race relations
7/64	Conservatives ask bishop to remove Jones
8/64	Bishop takes no action
2/65	Jones goes to Alabama on Freedom March
3/65	Eleven families leave the church
4/65	Men's Club decides to go to bishop again
5/65	Present

Have the group draw a chart that shows the centers of power and who leads them within the church and describe how and through whom they communicate with each other. Chart III is a fictitious example of a "centers of power" chart. Some churches prefer to use a regular organization chart to show these power relationships, and include on it both formal and informal relationships.

67572

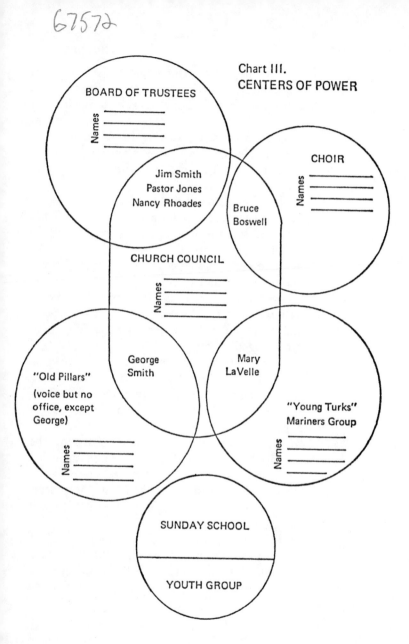

Chart III.
CENTERS OF POWER

BOARD OF TRUSTEES

Names

Jim Smith
Pastor Jones
Nancy Rhoades

CHOIR

Names

Bruce
Boswell

CHURCH COUNCIL

Names

George
Smith

Mary
LaVelle

"Old Pillars"

(voice but no
office, except
George)

Names

"Young Turks"
Mariners Group

Names

SUNDAY SCHOOL

YOUTH GROUP

Have the groups draw a force-field analysis of where the church currently stands with regard to the struggle. A force-field analysis is a chart with two parallel columns representing forces moving toward change (called driving forces) and forces resisting change; the relative strength of each is indicated—for example, by arrows of varying length. See Chart IV.

The values of this kind of methodology are:

It tends to get the conflict acted out or projected for all to see, and it immediately involves others in helping to clarify it.

It is more economical (saving time, energy) than questionnaires and interviews.

It allows for impressions and feelings to be aired as well as opinions and ideas.

It can be helpful to those who have a difficult time expressing their ideas.

The problems with this methodology are:

It tends to be impressionistic.

It depends on the information from those who show up for the meeting. Those who choose not to appear are not heard from.

Some of the instruments mentioned above may be perceived as "freaky" and can cause increased resistance.

If there is little trust in the group or the process and people are afraid to speak, the method will not work.

It is difficult to assess whether or not the silent majority has been captured by the outspoken leadership of the church. That is, a few people may be able to express an opinion well, get the

approval of the leadership (and the referee), but
their opinion may not be understood or agreed
upon by the large number of persons.

It is quite possible that the real concerns will not
emerge through this method, especially if the group
facilitators are not cautious with regard to spending all
the time "chasing rabbits" and not tending to business.
Knowing whether one has "real" concerns is largely an
intuitive process. The referee will have to keep checking

Chart IV. FORCE-FIELD ANALYSIS

*Proposed change: First Downtown Church
should move to the suburbs.*

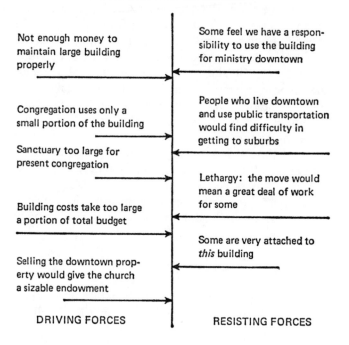

Not enough money to
maintain large building
properly

Some feel we have a responsibility to use the building
for ministry downtown

Congregation uses only a
small portion of the building

People who live downtown
and use public transportation
would find difficulty in
getting to suburbs

Sanctuary too large for
present congregation

Lethargy: the move would
mean a great deal of work
for some

Building costs take too large
a portion of total budget

Some are very attached to
this building

Selling the downtown property would give the church
a sizable endowment

DRIVING FORCES   RESISTING FORCES

out (testing) his intuition with as many as possible as he goes along.

We would suggest that a good deal of time be spent establishing the objectives of each small group with those who are in that group. Time should also be spent getting ownership of the process that will be used. By "getting ownership" we mean helping persons to participate in deciding what shall be done and how it shall be done. Thus, they will know why they are doing it and what value it will have for them. If what is done is not clear, there will be resistance to the methodology and useful data will not be generated.

Furthermore, we would strongly suggest taking plenty of time to train small-group facilitators before the actual group processes begin. If, however, no one is perceived as neutral and the decision is made to bring in outside facilitators, it would be preferable not to have group leaders at all. Training advocates to be group leaders may appear as "stacking the deck," unless opponents are used as coleaders. We do not recommend this procedure because it usually results in a debate rather than a data-gathering session.

Finally, as we have mentioned before, adequate time should be taken for meetings. In a voluntary association only rarely is it necessary to make a decision on any given night. Take time to get agreement on the problem-solving process and let everyone examine and modify its component parts.

Direct Observation

Finally, a quite appropriate way to gather information on what is happening in a particular conflict is by direct observation. It is very difficult for those who are materially affected by the conflict to be objective in their observations, but if neutral parties can be identified, this can be an excellent method.

This process requires an observer to witness the church at work (or in conflict) and to make note of the *behavior* that he sees. He then feeds back the observations he has of *what people are doing* that, in his opinion, tends to continue the conflict and to obstruct the resolution of the conflict in a healthful and productive way. We have been careful to use the words "behavior" and the phrase "what people are doing." It is almost never helpful to try to describe *why* people are behaving as they are, nor it is helpful to try to analyze what their behavior means. An observer can be most helpful when he aids persons to become aware of what they are doing and what effect that action may have on those with whom they work.

The value of using this method is that it can put real behavior in perspective. The problem with this method is that it is more difficult to get "ownership" of the data. That is, an observer's reflections "belong" to the observer and it takes a good deal of convincing to help others see things as the observer does. Direct observation, in other words, is a method that tends to increase resistance toward the observer because it is incumbent upon him to interpret his data. The other methods, mentioned above, can be interpreted by the parties affected and do not produce as much resistance.

9

Analysis of Data

Once the data have been collected from all the sources, they must be put in some kind of form that is understandable to everyone concerned. We strongly recommend against putting the information in a written, formal report, primarily because these reports don't get read and they are rarely understood. A summary of the findings should be presented by the referee using a blackboard and chalk or newsprint and a felt-tip pen. Presenting the data this way makes it seem less formal and formidable as well as being open to challenge and change.

Categorizing the information is always helpful. Putting it up as "information relevant to the substance of the debate," "information relevant to personal feelings," and "information relevant to the fight's context" will help persons give meaning to the information that they have. Then one can write down proposals as to what the group might do in the light of the information. When we are acting as referee, we prefer to follow this procedure in analyzing the data: Ask all the affected parties to attend a "feedback meeting" at a given time and place. The referee chairs this meeting and explains to the people what he understands to be the information from the data-gathering by pointing to all the data on the newsprint and giving supporting detail to substantiate each point. After he has explained the data the referee asks if his understanding of the information is correct or if it needs to be modified or added to in any way. Usually it does need to be modified somewhat, and the group changes the information until most of the persons present agree that it is a *fairly* accurate description of the situation. (Asking for an absolutely accurate description is asking for trouble. We find that general agreement is more important at this point than making sure that every "i" is dotted and every "t" crossed.)

The purpose of gathering this information is to help all the parties who are affected by the conflict to understand what is going on and how they will all be a part of the solution rather than continue to be a part of the problem. Therefore it is quite important that plenty of time is taken for all persons to share in the analysis of the conflict situation and to have a hand in modifying it to meet their specifications of satisfaction. At this stage the referee may find that some persons require some issues to be written using language and turns of phrase that most people in the group would not ordinarily be comfortable with. The key here is that the situation gets stated and restated over and over again, first in one kind of jargon and then in another until everyone has a common understanding of the same problems.

It will do the conflict managers (referees and advocates alike) no good whatsoever to be working on different problems even though the people are using the same

Fear of Impending Doom

Here is an example of such an experience. We were
called in to help manage a conflict that had developed
in a local church on the issue of whether to renovate
the church building. As we gathered the data, we found
that every person (with one highly marginal exception)
wanted to renovate the church and do it now. They were
afraid, however, that they might not have enough money
in the future to cover the payments even though they
had plenty at the present time. Furthermore, they were
afraid that there might be some people who would not
approve of the idea of using the church's money on
paint, carpeting, and a new parking lot. In fact, what
was troubling the people was the *possibility* of conflict.
Their concern was about what might happen if they
acted, rather than what in fact was going on at the
present time. This is what we call the "fear of impending doom" syndrome. The conflict is with a future possibility and not with anything that is currently happening.
In this kind of situation, what one needs to use are
more planning and decision-making techniques. This
is not a conflict situation, and conflict strategies for
solution would be inappropriate.

Fear of impending doom is sometimes felt by just one
person. Somehow, somewhere in a local church there
will emerge a graduate, experienced, credentialed *doomsayer*. His (or perhaps their) job will be to frighten
everybody to petrification every time there is the possibility of acting. When the idea of a coffeehouse for
teen-agers is being explored, the doomsayers encourage
the whole church to worry about bringing the wrong
"element" into the youth group. When the refurnishing

of the parlor is discussed, the church is reminded that the financial situation doesn't look too firm, and when the subject of capital punishment or of prison reform is mentioned, the pastor and others are reminded that continuing discussion of the matter might offend someone. The future, for the doomsayers, is seen to be without hope and the present without grace. They can generate substantive and interpersonal conflict situations and often rule the day. The rest of the congregation goes around with internalized, intrapersonal conflict ("I wish I had the guts to stand up to that doomsayer") and a feeling of dissatisfaction that they "aren't doing anything." When the congregation confronts the doomsayers, there is a real possibility of conflict, but when the doomsayers are allowed to "win," we do not have conflict, only dissatisfaction.

Withdrawal

A second kind of nonconflict situation occurs when a faction is allowed to win a decision and the rest of the people (whether a majority or a minority) go along with that faction's decision. There is no conflict unless at least two of the sides are willing to do battle. When one side pouts in the corner and will not confront the opposition, this is not a conflict situation. When a faction walks out and doesn't stick it out and fight, doesn't try to organize its troops, doesn't stand up for what it believes or wants, there is no conflict. Until there are at least two forces trying to occupy the same space at the same time, there is no conflict.

Strategies that are appropriate for managing the unhappiness, dissatisfaction, or apathy of the members might be to help those committed to noncombat organ-

ize and articulate their position so that the conflict will
be made manifest and therefore manageable. Or, in some
cases, one might simply help people to adjust to the
situation of being powerless.

Lack of Planning

A third kind of nonconflict situation existed where the
minister and most of the key lay people were quite unhappy about the lack of participation on the part of
most of the other members of the church. They were
angry and dissatisfied because of what others were not
doing in the church. It is true that anger and ill feelings
were present in the situation, but this rancor was not a
function of conflict, either interpersonal or substantive.
The fact that nothing was getting done led to a few
manifestations of interpersonal conflict, but the major
problem was one of poor planning, lack of processes
that would include substantial participation of the
congregation in planning and implementation, and poor
organizing on the part of the leadership.

Lack of adequate planning for congregational participation is one of the most common causes of grief in
churches. When a broad base of participants is not included in the planning and has little say as to whether
the planning is appropriate to its needs—whether they
think the methods for meeting those needs are appropriate or whether they appreciate the way the processes
are administered—many of the feelings of conflict will
be present. Indeed, it is often the case that where there
has been little or no planning that includes the congregation, no one is sure what the church's goals and
objectives are. This leads to confusion and to the feeling
of conflict simply because of the uncertainty about in-

dividual need fulfillment and individual roles in meeting the expectations of others. Participatory planning, including goal-setting and plans for implementing the goals, is a better way to handle this problem.

ROLES MUST BE CLARIFIED

If the referee and the group determine that they are in a situation where there is no conflict but other problems are present, we would suggest that the problem-solving outline in Chapter 14 be followed. First, talk about and agree on the new roles that will be called for in the newly understood situation. Especially, the role of referee should be dispensed with. For a person to stay in this role is tantamount to asking that others be antagonists. Therefore, if the group wishes to maintain the services of an objective outsider, it ought to redefine his role as a process consultant or facilitator. On the other hand, it may also be appropriate for the person who was functioning as referee to function as one of the group at this point or to stop working with the group entirely. Once roles have been clarified, then it will be possible to follow the problem definition and problem-solving process described in Chapter 14.

11

Second-Stage Contract

In the preceding chapter we examined what might be done in the situation where the referee and the group or groups decide that, though real dissatisfaction and pain were present, it was a nonconflict situation. The rest of the book will be looking at those situations where conflict is present.

Once the determination has been made that conflict is present, a second-stage contract must be made between the referee and the group he is working with. The second-stage contract should include all the elements covered in Chapter 4, where conflict management without a referee was discussed. Briefly, this means that the group should now, with the referee, agree on the process that it will go through, the decision rule that will be used, the group's goals, and a time by which it intends to accomplish its goals.

We cannot overemphasize the importance of this phase of the management process. It is not only important in establishing your credibility as a referee, but it is also important in making sure that expectations are not out of line with what it is possible for you or anybody else to produce in the situation. In addition, it begins to allow all the parties to have more experiences (with the referee and with each other) that do not end up in hurt feelings, anger, and tears.

We feel that in every situation, it is a good idea to put this contract in writing. That doesn't mean that one must have a printed form which all parties sign. The referee may simply write the agreements on newsprint or he may write a letter to each of the groups involved, outlining what he understood to have come out of the contracting meeting as to what the parties expect to accomplish, how they will do it, when, where, and so on. This will give all the parties a chance to reexamine their expectations and to make sure that they all have a basis for beginning to work.

One of the things we like to do at the first meeting after we have established this contract is to provide some input to all the groups involved, assuring them that conflict is not a sign of an unhealthy group, that conflict has many positive functions (as we mentioned in the first part of this book), and that we have been through many experiences like the one they are currently undergoing and, though not all encounters were successful in eradicating the conflict, in no case did we make matters worse. A good deal of guilt is usually present for being in conflict in the first place, and a referee should attempt to do what he can to assure the participants that they are not wrong or unchristian for being in such a situation. Furthermore, the group will have a lot of reticence with an outsider there, especially since they are

12

Interpersonal Conflict

The reality we usually experience in church fights is that one cannot neatly sort out substantive conflict from interpersonal conflict situations. Many conflicts begin with substantive issues and then develop into interpersonal battles. In other situations we find that interpersonal or emotional conflicts quickly lead to the discovery of issues that can be used to carry the freight of the emotional clash.

The fundamental distinction we are making here is that some conflict in churches has, at its root, issues of substance that are contested among competing groups. Other conflict is, however, primarily interpersonal or has a heavy interpersonal component; that is, it is essentially between individuals rather than between issues of substance. Of the greatest value, in our opinion, in seeking to find theory and strategies in managing interpersonal conflict is the work of Eric Berne and those of his school of transactional analysis. For the purpose of this book, we will mention here only briefly some of the symptoms of interpersonal conflict, some conditions for being able to manage it, and one process that we have found to be effective (borrowed and modified from transactional analysis) in handling interpersonal conflict situations.

SYMPTOMS OF INTERPERSONAL CONFLICT

During the data-gathering of the conflict management process, one or all of four common behaviors that are probably symptomatic of interpersonal conflict between persons in the congregation may be noticed.

The first of these symptoms of interpersonal conflict is *withdrawal:* where persons prefer to avoid each other and not be at the same meeting with certain other individuals, or where people have little to say to each other.

Another symptom of interpersonal conflict is *rationalization:* where one party tries to explain the other party's behavior or attitude by some theory (usually psychological) that puts the other down and does not allow him to have a legitimate claim on the situation. A common expression that we have heard at church meetings is, "He is (they are) too young to understand; give him a few years and he will see things as we do (the truth)." Or, almost as often, "He's too old to understand where it's at today."

A third very common behavior that is a symptom of interpersonal conflict is profuse *denial that any conflict exists.* We attended a church meeting recently where the entire agenda was devoted to short and long speeches on (*a*) how much Christians *should* love one another, (*b*) how much Christian love one has in his heart, and

(c) why one *shouldn't* express differences of opinion in church. We thought the ladies and gentlemen did protest too much!

A fourth common symptom is *fight behavior*, which manifests itself in long shouting matches, name-calling, organizing to get the pastor fired, and other behaviors of which the reader is probably well aware if he has been motivated to read this far in this book.

CONDITIONS FOR MANAGING INTERPERSONAL CONFLICT

Three conditions are absolutely necessary before interpersonal conflict can be successfully managed. The first is that both sides must be willing to "work" the interpersonal component. To illustrate this point we refer to one of our conflict management failures rather than to one of our successes. We were asked to help a pastoral relations committee to deal with their minister. All parties agreed verbally (note *verbally*) that we should have a retreat with the pastor and the committee and that we would deal with all relevant factors (feelings, facts, and next steps). When we began the one-day meeting we encouraged the members of the committee to express their feelings openly about the church, about each other, and about the pastor. The committee members were at first reluctant to do this, but finally got into the swing of it and were quite candid about their recent dissatisfaction with certain things the minister had been doing and the way he had been treating them. After about two hours of true confession, one of the members of the committee asked the pastor to express his views just as candidly about them. The pastor's response was that he was not willing to do so and that he thought the whole discussion was unnecessary. He then made a proposal about how the budget should be raised for the following year. This, of course, infuriated the committee all the more, for they had candidly revealed themselves to the pastor and he was unwilling to be reciprocally open and honest. This caused an increase in hard feelings that hurt matters rather than helped them.

Second, it is necessary for all parties to recognize that feelings are facts and are relevant to the management of the conflict. Feelings must be a part of the discussion and must be considered appropriate to examine and manage just as the substantive issues are. Without the recognition of the importance of feelings as well as facts, methods, goals, and values, and without some attempts to air these feelings and deal with them, there cannot be any significant change in the quality of relationship.

Third, both sides must perceive that it is safe to expose their feelings. It is a matter of fact that people do not reveal their feelings to those they perceive to be a threat. A pastor may be angry at the board but will not tell them so unless he feels it is safe to do so. He is more likely to direct these feelings to a safe target (ask his wife). A subordinate may not feel that it is safe to reveal his feelings to his boss but he may reveal them to his bartender or to some other disinterested person. Therefore, before trying to get people to deal with their feelings with each other, the necessary groundwork must be laid to help all parties perceive that this will be a safe time and place to deal with feelings and other relevant factors that are a part of the interpersonal conflict.

Interpersonal Conflict Management Process

For dealing with interpersonal conflict, we usually use the following procedure. The first phase is the establishment of an interpersonal *contract*. Each party must understand what he is getting into, what might come out of the experience, what is expected of him, and what will be expected of the others involved. In other words, all parties must agree to the goals of the process, the methods to be used, and the style of implementation. Without this, each can (and should) only be defensive and will not be ready to try to improve the relationship.

The second phase has to do with internal *clarification*. It is imperative that before conflict (whether it be interpersonal or substantive) can be worked, each person must be as aware as possible of what is going on within himself and within the other person. Specifically, we feel that it is important to identify all those feelings and experiences which each person thinks is relevant to the problem, and then we can work at (1) helping each individual to clarify his own understanding of the problem and (2) helping each individual to comprehend the other's understanding.

This process of clarification, in transactional analysis, is called the "trackdown." For our purposes, we have modified it and use it in this form:

1. Describe exactly how you hurt.
2. Describe who or what caused it and when it started.
3. Why did he, she, they, or it do it?
   On purpose? By accident?

The third step has to do with *differentiating the issues*. Once each party has a sense of the entire picture, we want to begin to name and to analyze the various issues that are a part of the problem.

Fourth, we will want to *clarify what each party wants* out of the situation. It is not only important to know what the elements of the conflict are, but the goals of the individual with regard to that conflict should also be clear. Often the parties feel that it is sufficient for each to let the other know (in a safe setting) how he feels about the other, and sometimes each party has very specific needs that he wants the other to meet (e.g., "Will you please cease and desist from saying 'Amen' in worship services, it is annoying to me"). What is important here is that each has an understanding of what he wants and what the other wants, so that they can move to the final step.

The final step is establishing a *process* whereby the parties can work the issue and then implement a decision-making process that will accomplish what each wants from the situation. The process can be seen as this kind of development: listening, sorting, planning, and problem-solving.

Notice that the process moves from establishing communication (listening) to collaborating (sorting and planning) and then, *after the fighters have had two experiences of succeeding at doing a task (sorting and planning) together*, actually working to accomplish the necessary resolution, boundary agreement, or reconciliation that the parties wish to accomplish. The two experiences of succeeding at a task are those of sorting and of planning how they will go about solving their problem.

This moves the antagonists from experiencing a feeling of fight to experiencing a feeling of collaboration and problem-solving, and the stage is set for the possibility (not the inevitability) of being able to solve a problem together.

In transactional analysis terms, this process is sometimes called "hooking" the Adult. Therapists of this school assume that we have three personality states out of which it is common for us to operate: the Parent, or our prejudging, blaming, righteous part; the Child, or our playful, creative, and sometimes pouting part; and the Adult, or our rational, analytical part. In conflict we are likely to be "taken over" by meanness (Child) or blaming (Parent), our whining and crybaby side (Child) or self-righteousness (Parent). Neither our Parent nor our Child is very competent at managing conflict. They both demand to win, and neither functions as a good problem solver. In interpersonal conflict, we want to get out of either the Parent or the Child mode in order to solve problems, and it is therefore necessary for the referee to help each party try to "hook" (be taken over by) his Adult. Through the process of listening, sorting, planning, and problem-solving, the parties have the greatest possibilities of actually succeeding at pulling themselves out of their childish and blaming ego states. Thus, our major stategy for managing interpersonal conflict is to use all means available for giving the antagonists new experiences of doing collaborative work together in an ego state that wants to solve problems rather than an ego state that cannot solve problems. Specific interventions that the referee may choose to use to help persons get into or stay in the Adult ego state include the double column method, Rogerian repetition, stop the music, and catharsis.

The Double Column Method

Sometimes, in the midst of the problem-solving process, it may appear that things are going to fall apart again and that control of the situation will be completely lost. When that happens, ask each party to write down those factors which favor a particular solution *and* those factors which are negative toward it. This will help the individuals to get out of their role of defender or attacker and to attempt to become more critical and less polemical.

Rogerian Repetition

This method is named after Carl Rogers, who, we understand, invented it. When two persons are having a heated discussion that is going nowhere, the referee intervenes and suggests that no one speak until he has restated to the previous speaker's satisfaction that person's last statement. This process must continue and be used with all the participants, until the various parties are beginning to hear what the others are saying and to take it into account before they make further suggestions. Thus, when the first speaker says he does not like a certain solution because of A, B, and C, then the second speaker must repeat to the first speaker's satisfaction the essence of his remarks. After the second speaker has repeated the first's point of view and has stated his own, then, and only then, may a third person speak, and, of course, he must repeat the second speaker's point of view (but not the first speaker's) before he can make his point, and so on.

Stop the Music

Another intervention we use quite often is to ask all the parties to hold their arguments for a few moments while the whole group analyzes what has been happening up to this point. What is sought here is a description of the process, a description of behavior and the effect of behavior on others in the group. This helps to bring the conversation into the here and now. It allows everyone to become aware of what is happening to the members of the group, to be aware of the effect of one person's behavior on others, and to "re-group," that is, to figure out what one is going to do next, not only in his own self-interest but also in the interest of the group.

Catharsis

On rare occasions it is sometimes appropriate to encourage persons to "let it all hang out," or to tell another person or persons those things which they have been bottling up inside themselves for a long time. Here the person who has it all stored inside may be encouraged by the referee to say fully what he has on his mind.

This method is often appropriate where an associate minister has been afraid to tell the senior minister of his dissatisfactions and feelings about the way the senior minister does things. Just saying it can be a very meaningful and "unblocking" experience for the junior minister.

Such an experience would not be a good idea if the senior minister were especially insecure or would use the associate's revelations against him or would not be just as candid with the associate as the associate has been with him. It would also be inappropriate to use this method where persons have had little or no experience in open and honest confrontation. Such practice at leveling should come under circumstances that have low risk and the possibility of the development of a healthy relationship. Therefore this method should be used with caution only where one feels that the persons who use it will be quite likely to benefit from it.

Miscellaneous Interventions

Other tricks of the trade that may help to lower the power of interpersonal conflict are:

> Ask speakers to address their remarks to specific persons rather than blaming an unknown and general "they."
>
> Limit speakers to one point at a time.
>
> Ask persons to sit in a circle and not in rows, so that they must speak to faces rather than to backs of heads.
>
> Allow persons to speak only for themselves.
>
> Ask persons to focus their remarks on describing behavior rather than "put downs." Thus: "You monopolized the conversation" or "You spoke ten minutes out of the last fifteen," is preferable to "You're a loudmouth."

It means that resources which could be put to other uses must be directed toward figuring out what to do each time that IT might be discussed or come up in a meeting. The church staff and the church leadership must take time in planning how to get around the issue and keep it from becoming an open battle.

At times it may be appropriate to use avoidance strategies. When a group has a very short time in which to accomplish certain tasks, it is often appropriate to avoid issues that the group feels are extraneous or not materially relevant to the current task. For example, it may happen that the church heating system quits working irreparably in the middle of winter and a decision must be made as to what to do for worship next Sunday. Now this decision is not going to affect the whole future of the church; it is not going to establish a policy or practice that is to last forever. Therefore it is not necessary to have a complete long-term analysis of the problem with all factions of the church present. In fact, bringing traditional enemies into the decision-making process for this short-term question may not be very wise. In such a case, one may avoid the conflict and make the decisions with those with whom he can make the decision. Then, with regard to the longer-term issues ("How will we finance another heating system?" and "Where will we meet during the winter if it takes a long time to get a new system?"), one can use other strategies to make these decisions.

Another situation in which the time is short and it may be appropriate to avoid conflict could be when one has the opportunity to organize a caucus at a denominational annual convention that will make resolutions with regard to U.S. foreign policy. The caucus has only a few hours to prepare its resolutions at the convention in between other regularly scheduled meetings. In this kind of situation it might be the wisest course of action to get people into that caucus who can collaborate and thus come to a decision quickly. Avoid the people who are going to be blockers in the accomplishment of the group's task. One needs people who will challenge and raise questions as to the group's product, but let those who generally oppose the group's aims and purposes be avoided. They won't help get the task done over the short haul.

Other situations in which it might be appropriate to evade open conflict would be where conformity is required in order to accomplish a task, as in a situation where it may be to a group's advantage to present a united front in order to gain some advantage over another group.

Further, we would try to avoid conflict in a group if we perceived that the individuals involved were particularly fragile and insecure. Our experience, however, is that people are not usually as fragile and insecure as they make themselves out to be, nor are they as delicate as our fantasies might perceive them to be. In other words, most persons can really take a lot, and to confront them with regard to their stand on the way money is raised in the church or on one's perception of them as a blocker is not going to mean suicide or emotional devastation. It probably will mean pain, but not collapse. Indeed, it is possible that it will bring new insight and growth.

Nonetheless, there are a few rare situations where the individuals are fragile and insecure, and conflict should not be dealt with immediately. In the situation where there has been a tragic loss in the church and people are going through the grief process, it is usually not appropriate to use confrontation strategies. Further, we have found that some churches seem to attract particularly helpless people. With this kind of group, direct confrontation methods would probably significantly cripple rather than enhance growth possibilities for the individuals and for the group as a whole.

Moreover, in those groups where there is high likelihood of group disintegration or violence, we would also recommend avoidance of the conflict as the initial strategy. Until there are some control possibilities, it would seem to us unwise for the individuals to fight it out. In some cases the conflict will have escalated beyond controversy over the issues to a point where each faction views the other as inhuman or depraved. Under such conditions it is highly unlikely that either side will see any reason why it should not use violence or other inappropriate conflict management methods. In such a predicament the person interested in change will have to work within the offending factions in order to de-escalate before he seeks to use the other conflict management strategies suggested in this book.

Finally, it may be appropriate, as a management strategy, to evade certain facets of the conflict and to choose to start on another area of the conflict. We find ourselves in this kind of circumstance quite often when we wish to focus first on the interpersonal elements of the conflict before moving on to the substantive issues. Here we use various strategies to avoid the substantive issues until we have allowed the group to vent their feelings of hostility and express those feelings which they assumed it was necessary to keep bottled up inside themselves. With one church in a small town, we began the conflict management strategy by asking the three factions to make a list of the things about the other groups that bothered them (we will describe this method in detail later on). Whenever anyone wanted to discuss a substantive issue, we let the person say what he had to say and then quickly replied, in the role of referee: "We'll get to that later. Right now let's try to focus on some of the feelings that are getting in the way of accomplishing our work." Here, the intent was to surface certain elements of the conflict and to avoid others until a more appropriate time.

Although on certain occasions it may be appropriate to avoid dealing with conflict, there are a number of risks in the evasion. The major risk is that most of one's energy will be spent avoiding the conflict and very little strength will be left to accomplish tasks. Avoiding conflict reduces the total creativity of the group. New ideas will be few and far between. Old ideas will not get reexamined. Indeed, someone has said that when everybody is thinking in the same way, no one is thinking very much.

The major strategy for avoiding conflict in church groups is simply to reduce the frequency of encounters that the antagonists have with each other. Try to keep them apart. Sometimes that means that someone functions as a messenger. Sometimes it means that virtually no communications go on between the cliques at all. Only those who must be at meetings are invited to them, and, where church bylaws so provide, outsiders or observers or guests are not welcome at the meetings. Other methods, of course, are striking the offending items from the agenda of the meetings, or placing them at the end of a long agenda and stalling during the first part of the

evening on inconsequential matters so there isn't time
to deal with that part of the agenda. Another way of
avoiding conflict is to give data-gathering tasks related
to the conflict to committees that will not do their work.
Without these committees' reports it will not be possible to continue the decision-making process.

REPRESSING THE CONFLICT

Notice that we did not use the word "controlling" or
"stopping" the conflict to describe this strategy. It is
not possible for anyone to control or to stop a conflict.
It may be possible by one ploy or another to inhibit it
temporarily. But to put chains on it at one moment is
surely to guarantee that it will break those chains at
some time in the future. By repressing the conflict, we
mean any use of whatever power the referee or church
leader may have to put down (probably temporarily),
or quell, or check the emerging conflict. It means to try
to hold the conflict back from the overt attention of the
group or the individuals within it or to redirect the
group's attention if the conflict happens to emerge.

In order to repress conflict, it is necessary for the re-
pressor to have some kind of power in the group. It is
not possible for a person with no influence in a group,
or no authority, sanctions, or other coercive means, to
have an effect on the emergence of the conflict. The conflict in itself has great power, and it will take power to
put the conflict down. Therefore (and let all potential
referees beware), unless one has the authority or is perceived to have skills that can be helpful to the group,

there is no way he can repress conflict that the group does not wish him to repress.

In another unhappy experience that we had, we were asked by one group within a church to help them manage a conflict. Upon arriving at the first meeting with all parties present, we were politely but potently made ineffective by a lack of interest in our ideas and no perception that we might have anything to offer. Finally, after an attempted first-stage contract meeting, two thirds of the group voted in favor of a motion that we not be invited back. For us to help that group to do anything (let alone try to repress anything it was already doing) would simply have been impossible. In order for this strategy to work, one must have some power within the group.

Assuming that one does have the requisite power, when would it be appropriate to attempt to use repression? The primary occasion for using such a strategy would be in an emergency. If the conflict is going to mean the immediate loss of something that the whole church values, if it is obvious that the conflict will lead to an unproductive end, one might attempt to repress the conflict. In other words, if the costs of the conflict will be greater than its merit or whatever may be produced from it, then repression is warranted. As we indicated with regard to avoidance strategies, however, it is usually the case that what may seem to lead to a costly experience may indeed not be the case.

One's fear of conflict and the norms of our culture reinforce the hasty assessment that any conflict will be more costly than it is worth. But we have learned through experience and study that this widely acknowledged cultural norm is not true. The cost of conflict avoided or repressed is usually greater than the cost of conflict faced and dealt with. The lingering agony of the unresolved concerns, the energy that is sapped in containing feelings or denying needs, and the clever games that must be played in order to keep the organization barely alive are rarely worth the short-term pain of coping with difference. However, in some rare situations, where the costs may be higher than the risk of repressing the conflict (as in the case of the great likelihood of violence), repression may be an appropriate strategy.

The use of repression may also be appropriate in the more likely event that the issues are not related to the organization or its tasks. Sometimes people try to get a local church to do something that is not in the interest of the mission of the church but only in the interest of their own personal gain. In a Presbyterian church we know, one woman tried to get the session to allow her to put on a reducing course using the church facilities and charging participants so that she could make a profit. No one was interested in doing this, but she pressed her case. Since there were other matters more urgent, she was encouraged not to continue to push her own interest, but in the interest of church unity to forget it.

The risks in the use of repression are the same as those in the use of avoidance. If the differences are important, feelings will find a way to be expressed within the organization. What is most likely to happen is that the hostile feelings will be expressed indirectly, that is, not at the cause of the discomfort but at some safe target. For example, if one were ridiculed or ignored every time he raised a certain issue at a church board meeting, it is quite likely that instead of taking his feelings out on the board members who are directly causing him the pain, the board member is more likely to take out his built-up aggression on the minister or on the head of the Christian education committee or on some other target considered by him to be safe. Some people displace their aggressions and vent them on targets outside the church, e.g., after a particularly bad church meeting an employer may take out his anger on his subordinates or a husband may take it out on his wife.

What are some of the strategies that one can use to repress conflict in the church? The most common is the continual emphasis and harping on loyalty, cooperation, teamwork, and Christian fellowship. Whenever someone raises an issue that may look to others in the church like dissension, the immediate tactic that is employed is to remind the "offender" that this is a *Christian* fellowship, which means that differences are not allowed. Or lengthy speeches (filibusters) on koinonia will be heard from the pastor, lay leaders, and the president of the women's society at the hint of a new idea or different approach to fulfilling the church's mission.

Another effective repressive tactic is to focus on the costs of any given action. When an idea for change comes up, the church leadership is reminded of the straits the budget is in and the inability of the church to survive if it loses one more member.

A better technique, to our way of thinking, is to name the difficulties of dealing with the conflict at this time and then to get the affected parties to evaluate temporary control possibilities until the emergency or other need for repressive action has passed. This process tends to be less manipulative, and it allows the whole group to examine alternative strategies for determining their own destiny. We particularly like this method because even when there is no emotional reconciliation at the time, with everyone participating in developing better coping techniques (even though temporary), all the parties are likely to feel more in control of their environment and less controlled by it.

Escalating the Conflict

When we speak of escalating the conflict we mean making the conflict a contest, that is, helping all the parties to equip themselves properly to try to win the fray. This is the strategy that is most often used in churches. The whole notion of making decisions by voting is a contest strategy. At the heart of the contest is the assumption that superior power is measured by a majority vote. Immature tactics that are often used to implement the strategy usually include sermonizing, withholding of affection, special pleading, bombast, whining, cajoling, trickery, half-truths, cataclysmic visions of the future, waiting to see how the pastor votes, rumor campaigns (via the telephone the next day or in parking-lot discussions after the meeting), asking the bishop or the district superintendent (depending on the size of the church) to intervene, or threatening to withdraw membership (more risky, the person may not be missed).

These contest tactics are not exactly what we would recommend as very mature means for a conflict strategy. Sometimes it is appropriate, however, to escalate the conflict using more sophisticated means. Escalation is appropriate when there is genuine polarization in the church, whether it be single-pole or multi-pole, and there is mutual motivation to work the issues. This means that the people in the church feel that it would be helpful to continue the contest in order to obtain a clarification of the issues and to help individuals and groups make up their minds as to which side they are going to take. A commonly practiced example of this kind of behavior is the organizing and debating on resolutions that are going to be presented on the floor of a denomination's convention. It is quite appropriate to try to line up as many votes as possible beforehand. It is quite appropriate to make as persuasive a speech as possible in favor of your point of view (at the same time discrediting your opponent's position), and it is quite appropriate to carry out a parliamentary battle before the vote with regard to who is a delegate, what kind of motions can be put to the house, who is to be allowed to speak, and how long the debate shall last. But finally it comes down to a vote, and voting is the ultimate method used in most churches to resolve conflict. It is generally agreed that the minority will go along with the majority. Indeed, the majority wins.

If one is going to be the referee in a church contest, we would advise against his using the contest model of conflict resolution when he perceives that there is no mutual motivation to work the issue, or when there clearly is not a balance of power or powers. It weakens the group to have certain factions continually lose, especially in voluntary organizations. If there is little possibility of one group winning or even having a significant hearing, using a conflict strategy will only convince the obvious minority that their cause is fruitless, and it may motivate them to find a church home in more compatible surroundings. Further, as a referee, one should try to assess beforehand what the cost of the battle will be before it gets under way. Again, the victories won may be too costly for the church in the long run—even though truth will no longer be on the scaffold, and wrong no longer on the throne.

The risks involved in using this kind of strategy are primarily related to the issue of escalation. What may start out as a small contest on a rather small issue may develop into a large contest on numerous issues. We saw this happen in one church where a conflict emerged over whether the youth group would be allowed to go to a certain concert (to hear Pete Seeger). This issue was escalated a step at a time (but very quickly) into whether or not the youth minister would stay on the staff (he didn't).

Second, carrying out a contest, just as repressing it and avoiding it, takes tremendous energy from the individuals and groups within the church. If the contest is not ended after a reasonable amount of time, more time, energy, and resources will get tied up in maintaining one's position in the contest than in getting on with the mission of the church. Finally, it is possible that once a church has had a bad experience with a contest, it will be unable to face future conflict opportunity with any other strategy than that of repression or avoidance. In other words, the scars that may be left can be deep and abiding.

Nonetheless, if you have decided that your church is ready and able to use a contest strategy for the resolution of its differences, we would recommend that you

attempt to keep the contest within the following guide-
lines:

Be sure that all parties understand their roles. Nothing can be more devastating to a person than to perceive
himself as a friendly helper when all about him are
operating as tough battlers. Each advocate should see
his role in the particular contest as a contestant, and
should be helped to function in that role. It is a lot
easier to lose when one understands himself to be a
contestant than it is to lose when one perceives himself
to be everybody's friend.

Be sure that all parties understand the rules. Get the
rules clearly laid out before the battle begins and then
insist that everyone stick to them. Usually, the rules
have to do with who is a combatant (who can vote)
and who is not. When, who, and how the group will
make decisions are other questions on which policies
should be established for organizational functioning.

Seek to maintain a data base. Do all in your power
to keep all the parties focusing on behavior, facts, and
researchable assumptions. Whenever someone strays
from dealing with facts, that person needs to be helped
to redirect his oratory back to a data base. For example,
if the speaker says that 50 percent of the church will
leave if so and so happens, that fact can be checked out
with a survey after church on the following Sunday. Or
if he says that no one in the church likes the new choir
robes, that also can be checked out. But if the contestant says, "The National Council of Churches is infested
with pinkos," or, "The denomination has gone soft on
Communism," one cannot very well check those things
out. What can be done is to examine the National
Council of Churches' policy or position papers and

assess its compatibility with the church's policies and positions, but broad, sweeping, uncheckable declarations will not get one anywhere.

Get and keep large numbers of people participating. Allowing people to drop out of the contest or allowing the contest to drive people out will not help to resolve the conflict. When this happens, it is tantamount to avoiding the conflict. For a contest to work, the people must understand the issues, make a decision, and act on their decision. That is how the issues get clarified and dealt with.

Get agreement from all parties on the process that will be followed for the decision-making. This will help to give the people involved in the contest a feeling of control over what is happening and will take away that lost, impotent, and confused feeling that is often generated in the midst of a battle. This will also assure everyone that the battle will have a conclusion and that it will not go on forever and ever.

Finally, help the loser to save face. If the loser says he didn't really lose, because no one understood his position, let him say it. The winner doesn't have to win *and* destroy the loser. If the loser has to find some way to check out with others that he is O.K., opportunity ought to be given for him to do so. It is only human nature to deny that you really lost; so help the loser to be human. The victor needs no more than his victory; he doesn't need trophies or scalps.

As to the process that we would recommend for church fights using the contest model, whether it be the total church or just one of the task forces or committees, we advise that it be kept simple. The process should look something like this:

Allow time for each party to prepare its case.

Recommend that all parties find allies and support groups, and give them opportunity to do so.

Establish rules for the contest and a process for carrying it out with all parties affected by the battle.

Stick to the process.

Make a decision.

Help both the winner and the loser to reintegrate his functioning in the church.

14

Collaborative Strategies

The collaborative model for dealing with conflict is different from the three models (avoiding, repressing, and escalating) discussed in the preceding chapter in that it demands that all the parties to the fight be involved in determining what will be done and how it will be done. Everyone's resources will be used. Each person will have an opportunity to be heard. Each will have a part in shaping the final outcome and decision of the conflict.

At the heart of this strategy is the attempt to work through defensive and aggressive emotions that seem to take over individuals and groups in conflict and move on to rational decision-making. What happens when groups get into conflict is that the feeling of fight becomes so predominant that under the circumstances the only thing that makes sense is *to protect oneself*. When an individual feels that he is under attack, the only reaction that seems to be right as far as his emotional state is concerned is either to defend or attack (even if he can't defeat the scoundrels, he can at least besmirch their armor).

Now, this protective behavior actually gets in the way of managing what is going on. It blinds one. It makes one operate in an irrational way. Any good fight strategist knows that a good way to get control over his enemy is to get him mad, to put him on the defensive, to get him to focus on protection rather than on what is really happening in the situation. Once the opponent gets caught either in his defensiveness or in his anger, the antagonist will have the upper hand.

Further, as the fight—with its concomitant feelings—is maintained, the parties involved begin to believe that to fight is the only way to survive. Fighting becomes the only apparent way to cope with the situation. So, what the referee has to do is to allow the various parties in the battle to have a small taste of a more successful alternative strategy, which instinct and common sense tell them not to do. In other words, it is the referee's task to let the participants have small experiences of collaboration with the "enemy" and experience him in a state other than merely as *opposition*.

Do a Collaborative Analysis

Getting committed antagonists to collaborate may appear to be an impossible job, and when it is first attempted it will certainly seem hopeless. But it can be done, and this is the crux of the conflict management process. If the conflict manager or referee has been following the process outlined up to this point in the book, he has been doing a great deal to move the combatants in the direction of problem-solving and away from the feelings of fight—defensiveness and aggression. In addition to the data-gathering and contracting listed above we recommend that conflicted groups use the following methods to move toward collaborative problem-solving.

Factoring

Where the conflicted parties were not all involved in the data-gathering phase for one reason or another, it is quite appropriate to ask the various persons involved to do a collaborative analysis of what has brought the group to this point of conflict.

Factoring employs the data-gathering methods that were used with small groups, as mentioned in Chapter 8. Specifically, we like to use the time line, the centers of power, and the force field on most occasions. Other collaborative factoring tasks that we use are:

> Validating data collected by an outside party.
>
> Identifying and clarifying common and divergent objectives of all parties.
>
> Establishing a process by which we will carry on our problem-solving process.
>
> Achieving a common diagnostic understanding of what triggered the conflict, what tactics were used, and the consequences of the use of these tactics.

We think that factoring is usually most efficiently done when the group is divided into small groups, each of which discusses one of the tasks. After each small group finishes its time line or force-field analysis or other task, it reports to the whole group. The whole group is then allowed to modify the small group's analysis. Here again is an opportunity for the group to collaborate on a task, to work at getting a definition of the total church situation, and then to write problem statements.

We find that in this kind of situation it is best to have the small groups write the problem statements, each making its own list. Then should follow the procedure of merging the lists of the various groups. This can be done in one of two ways: either a subgroup made up of representatives from each small group can merge the lists into one list or the entire group can do it under the leadership of the referee. At this point, problem statements that are essentially the same should be made into one problem statement, so that when the group finishes merging the lists, it has accomplished two collaborative tasks: (a) it has made one list together and (b) it has taken two descriptions of the same problem and collaborated on making them one (this may be done several times in this phase).

The next phase is more difficult, but again it is essentially a collaborative one. Now that there is a list of problem statements that all agree are issues, it must be prioritized. The most important and the least important issues must be determined. It may be necessary at this point to determine whether to make this decision by vote or by consensus. Again, determining how to make the decision will be a collaborative task that the group can accomplish before it begins the task of prioritizing.

When the priorities are listed, the highest priority problem statements should be given to special task forces to work on. The task forces should be made up only of people who have been involved in the problem-solving process so far (except, possibly, for a neutral outside expert on technical issues if he is needed), representa-

tives from all affected groups, and a referee (if there is
still conflict over the issue). Each task force can then
go to work at problem-solving with its particular issue.

We like to begin to work one of the issues with a
single task force while the rest of the people in the
church observe this group at work. We call this the *fishbowl method*. The task force is in the center of the
room, inside the fishbowl, being observed by the rest of
the group, which is around the edges of the room. This
accomplishes several objectives simultaneously. It puts
participants on their best behavior (especially if they
are told that after a half hour we will ask the nonpartici-
pants to give the participants feedback on their behavior). It gives the referee an opportunity to model appropriate conflict management behavior—nondefensiveness,
problem-oriented rather than person-oriented conflict,
and direct confrontation of pertinent issues. Finally, it
allows the referee to practice with the group what the
appropriate steps are for a successful problem-solving
process.

After the "fishbowling," each task force can go to
work on its assigned task and report at a later date to
the appropriate boards and committees in the church
about their recommendations or accomplishments. Or if
there is still high mistrust, the small groups can report
to the large group before reporting to the appropriate
boards.

The Bug List Process

The bug list process begins by dividing the people
into groups, putting into the same group those who are
essentially compatible with each other vis à vis the current conflict. It will be important for the referee in his

initial data-gathering process to determine whether people are clear as to which side they are on. He may find that some are not clear as to whose camp they are in, and if this is the case, he will not be able to use this method. Assuming that people are clear as to which camp they are in, and assuming that there are no more than three groups, ask each homogeneous group to take two pieces of newsprint for every faction opposing it in the conflict management process. One of these pieces of paper should be labeled "How we see them" and the other should be labeled "How they see us." It will be important that each group has a name. Sometimes this is quite simple, e.g., the choir versus the board of trustees. At other times the conflict will be between groups that do not function with a title in the system, such as the liberals versus the conservatives, or "the people who want to move the church location" against "the people who want the church to stay where it is." We have found it helpful when encountering the latter situation to avoid using names or labels that contain within them value judgments or broad, sweeping commitments (like liberals and conservatives, or *status quo*). It is better to find as neutral and nonmeaningful a designation as possible, such as A and B. It may take a while for people to figure out whether they are in A or B, and the referee may have to help people to determine persons with whom they are most compatible. Still, we think that this method is superior to the process of giving people descriptive labels which they may have to justify or deny.

After the group has been divided into compatible subgroups, each list that they have made should be labeled "How A sees B" and "How A thinks B sees A."

Each group, by itself, is then encouraged to say and write down everything that comes to each person's mind. Negative, positive, and neutral comments are all appropriate. In the safety of a group in which one feels he is with his "own kind," it is hoped that the participants will be candid and complete in their descriptions of one another. The intention is to facilitate two-way communication and understanding by helping each group to reveal what is going on within itself and to seek to become sensitive to what is going on in the other groups.

After the lists are completed by all the groups, they should be posted where everybody can see them. We like to let people walk around and look at the lists and talk among themselves at this point. Then we have everyone sit down in a total group and one person in each group "walks through" his group's list. That is, they read and briefly clarify what they have written. If there are any questions of clarification (not argument or defense), they are encouraged at this time.

After each list has been walked through, we ask the original homogeneous groups to meet by themselves. The purpose of this second meeting is twofold: (1) It allows individuals to internalize what they have been hearing and (where necessary) to lick their wounds. (2) After discussion about their perceptions of themselves and of the others, the group can begin the task of identifying workable issues and writing problem statements.

In identifying the workable issues, the group is beginning to move from description to action. The first phase has allowed all sides to say what they had to say, it has opened the channels of communication in a highly structured manner, and no one has turned into a pillar of salt or has been irreparably damaged. This second phase starts the groups to work on specific problems and helps them focus on the means for arriving at collaborative solutions. After the problem statements are written, they should be agreed upon and prioritized, and then task forces can be determined which will be responsible for recommending specific solutions to the problems they were given.

Make a Concrete Problem Statement

Nothing will cause the group more grief than not being concrete about the problem. In one church the problem was described as "nobody sends their kids to Sunday school." This is not a specific problem.

Nonspecific problem definitions or statements make it very difficult to develop action plans to solve the church's problems. As long as members don't like what is going on and cannot be specific as to what it is they don't like, the pastor and the groups trying to solve the problems will be unable to do anything to solve them. Robert Bonthius, in describing the specific problem statements related to social issues, uses this kind of problem statement:

There really is no such thing as changing "the system." Although all systems of society are related, there are many systems. A group wishing to work for change in the way this society treats people has to move from sweeping judgments to specific faults. This means zeroing in on a system—for instance, the educational system, the welfare system, or the communications system. But it means more . . . [zeroing in] on problems within that system.

When a group is first asked to state the problems it is concerned about, individuals often come out with statements like, "Carping City is racist," "The mayor runs our town," "The police are hand in glove with the syndicate," "The Democratic party in our county is corrupt." Sweeping judgments. Quite probably true, but of little help if the group hopes to move beyond paralyzing rhetoric to effective action.

A good problem statement states the concern in one complete indicative sentence. The sentence contains at least three of the following items, preferably all four. The sentence tells:

Who is doing (or not doing) something;

What is being done (or not being done);

To whom it is being done (or not being done); and

When or *where* it is being done (or not being done).

When people settle down to write such a sentence, they can come up with statements like this:

The ten suburbs of Motion County have not allowed the Motion Metropolitan Housing Authority to build any public housing for the poor or the elderly of the county within their boundaries.

This statement tells who is doing what to whom, as well as when and where. Any group that wants action has to get definite, which literally means "set limits." Definiteness can empower a group. As one person commented, "This helped eliminate my feeling of powerlessness in the face of a multitude of problems." [1]

In a local church a problem statement might look like this:

During the past five years, the Christian Education Committee has not allowed any persons to teach

Sunday school except those who have a conservative theological point of view.

To illustrate this point even more specifically: We were working with a church in Southern California that was feeling pain at a number of points. After several data-gathering sessions with the official board of the church, its coordinating council, and the committee searching for a new pastor, it was determined that there were several problems that needed to be worked on separately, but action on any of them was to be approved by the whole church. Here is that church's list of problem statements.

The Pastoral Search Committee does not have a list of specific criteria for the selection of candidates that has been approved by the whole church.

The members of the church youth group feel that they are not allowed to make their own decisions as to who the youth group leader should be and as to what they will do and discuss at their meetings.

The chairmen of all the church committees do not have enough skill or understanding of small-group leadership and how to do problem-solving efficiently.

From this list of problem statements the church was able to move on easily through the last seven steps of the nonconflict problem-solving process.

The problem-definition stage will probably take a lot of time, the group will usually find it rather difficult, and one may encounter significant resistance at this point. Nonetheless, it is crucial for dealing with the issues. It is next to impossible to do anything about problems that are not specifically defined. Further, being able to define what the problem is may put it in a perspective that will enable the group to determine the amount of effort worth investing in its resolution.

Choose Task Forces to Develop Solutions

In both the factoring method and the bug list method it was indicated that task forces should be chosen to develop the solutions to the problems described in the problem statements. Task forces are recommended because they give persons in the church an opportunity to work with others in new and different relationships than those they may have been used to in the past. Where, for example, persons on the board of trustees are in regular conflict with members of the choir, a task force on the problem can be established that will allow persons to try to solve problems outside their old alliances and regular ways of doing things.

Therefore it is recommended that task forces be heterogeneous (include advocates from all parties), that they be given the task of recommending solutions to the problem they are assigned, that they be given a specific time by which they are to report their recommended solution(s) to the church or the appropriate board, and that they be relatively small in size (when possible). In this way it will be possible for the church to be working on a number of problems at the same time. Making the task forces small will enable the real work to go on, including everyone and listening to all points of view. Making the task forces heterogeneous will assure that the solutions do not favor one particular side or the other.

Set Objectives

Once the problems have been defined and the task forces selected, each task force should write its objectives. Usually an objective is a positive way of stating the problem. Instead of saying, "The Pastoral Search Committee has no criteria . . . etc.," an objective may be written: "That the Pastoral Search Committee will develop criteria by a certain date." The criteria for good objectives are that they:

State who will do the job.
State what specific action they will take.
State a time for completion.
State the extent to which the job will be done.
State who will be affected.

Thus an objective will state who will do what to whom, when, and to what extent. It is not always the case that each of these items needs to be included in an objective. In our opinion one does not have to indicate the number of criteria in the particular objective above. However, more often than not it is appropriate to indicate the quantity expected from any given objective. If an evangelism committee in a local church sets as its objective "to recruit new members for the church," it may be quite satisfied with one member a year, although other people might feel that fifty members a year would be both realistic and attainable. Therefore, in order to minimize misunderstanding and to be clear about what it is that a committee or a person is about, the objective should be clear as to amount as well as to who will be doing what.

Brainstorm Alternative Means to Achieve Objectives

Once the task force knows what it wants to do, it must determine how it will do it. Here we find brain-storming [2] to be an appropriate method. The brain-storming process is where all the participants search for *all* the ideas they can think of during a given period of time and write them down. The rules of good brain-storming are: All ideas are written down, none is re-jected; the atmosphere must be permissive and non-judgmental; the attempt is primarily to get a large quan-tity of ideas rather than just good ideas (the sorting is done later). Humor and free association are encouraged (in order to try to get at subconscious sources of crea-tivity).

After the task force has brainstormed its list of alter-native solutions, we feel that it is a good idea to leave the job alone for a while. Let the group go off and do something else, if it is an all-day meeting; or stop the process until the group meets at another time. During this incubation period other ideas may develop that ought to be recorded; indeed, they probably will develop.

Select a Solution

After the incubation period, select the feasible ideas. Note that we said "select the *feasible* ideas." This is not the point at which to determine the forever-and-ever solution. Here, one wants to look into the various pos-sible solutions. Then one can analyze the feasible ideas by gathering data as to what the consequences of any

WHO	TASK DESCRIPTION	WORK PLAN				PERSON HOURS	COST	PRODUCT
		Jan.	Feb.	March	April			
Director of religious education	Request curricula from six publishers	▌				40	$100.00	Six sets of curricula
Christian education committee	Develop criteria for curriculum selection	▌				10	- - -	List of criteria
Six Christian education subcommittees	Review curriculum and make recommendations			▌		40	- - -	Written recommendations
Christian education committee	From recommendations select a curriculum to present to total congregation				▌	20	- - -	One selection
Total congregation	Vote on Christian education committee's recommendation				▌	2	- - -	Order to buy material

Chart V. WORK PLAN

particular strategy might be in terms of cost, time required, acceptance of the solution by others, and the solution's appropriateness to the church's situation. Then, after one has done an analysis of several solutions, he can select the solution he wishes to implement.

Develop a Strategy

Once the task force is clear as to what it wants to do and how it will do this, it is sometimes helpful to chart the steps through which the group will move to accomplish the objective. Chart V illustrates such an instrument a group might use to chart the process for choosing a new Sunday school curriculum. The chart includes an indication of the number of hours that *each* person will put into each phase of the project. (It is not the total of every person's hours.) This will help everyone to be clear about what he is getting into in terms of a time commitment. The chart also includes a place to indicate the costs of a project. Most local church projects do not require this kind of budgeting, but denominational offices might find this a helpful tool, especially when they are figuring what it will cost to bring persons together from distant points to accomplish certain tasks.

IMPLEMENT AND EVALUATE

Finally, the task force should recommend its plans to the church or to the proper board for implementation and, then, evaluation. Evaluation is most important in helping to clarify what has been learned as to the best way to go about accomplishing problem-solving in the church. It is also helpful in getting the organization to look at issues other than just task accomplishment, issues such as individual development of committee members in the project, the growth of the committee itself, and the usefulness and importance of the committee to the mission of the church.

This problem-solving process has led the combatants through the necessary stages of development to arrive at mutually agreed upon solutions to problems. The key elements for success are: the referee's ability to keep control of the process, clarity as to where one is in the process, and the group's belief that the process will help it accomplish its goals. After the referee has led a group through the process several times, the group's skill and confidence in itself should increase to where it will be able to manage without the referee because it knows what to do and will not be devastated by differences.

NOTES

1. Robert Bonthius, "So—You Want to Change the System?" *Trends*, October, 1971.

2. For a full description of brainstorming, see Alexander Osborn, *Applied Imagination: Principles and Procedures of Creative Thinking* (Charles Scribner's Sons, 1953).

15

Conclusion

It has been our contention in this book that conflict in itself is not a bad thing. We have argued that conflict, though it may be experienced as painful and frightening, is the fire in which a healthy organization is tempered. On a number of occasions we have asked individuals in churches to tell each other what is currently happening in their lives where personal growth is taking place, and it is a rare occasion when someone will mention a non-conflict situation that is bringing growth to his life. More often we hear people describe the pressures of their jobs, new demands that their teen-age children are placing on them, or a struggle with their spouse as the kind of experience that is bringing strength, maturity, and growth to them as individuals.

This is not to say, however, that because some growth comes from conflict, all growth does; nor do we mean to imply that all conflict is growth-producing. Those persons or groups which live for conflict, it seems to us, are just as unhealthy as those which spend all their energy avoiding it.

In this book, we have attempted to argue that one mark of a healthy organization is that it can deal with conflict when it arises and that the conflict can bring with it growth. Further, the process of dealing with that conflict can be a collaborative one. The parties who are at odds—if there is any basis of consensus in the group—can become aware of how the conflict is managing them, rather than their managing the conflict, and they can begin to develop strategies that will help them achieve what it is they want in the organization.

Some readers may wish that we had provided short, magic, easy answers in this book that would have solved all their conflict problems. For us it was sometimes tempting to try to prescribe "solutions" that would have made conflict go away. But we think that panaceas (if we had any) would only give the reader another excuse to avoid conflict and miss the potential for growth that will be found in it.

Appendixes
and
Bibliography

APPENDIX I

How to Choose
an Outside Consultant

PROFESSIONAL BACKGROUND

Many excellent consultants to churches in conflict are not full-time consultants. Some are university professors, some are teachers, but many who competently do this work on a part-time basis have other occupations. The fact that a person does not do this full time should in no way deter you from considering him. However, we do recommend that you hire only people who have some professional accreditation. The fact that they have credentials from reputable accrediting agencies will show the reader that they are willing to be examined and tested by their peers. There are many accrediting organizations that are reputable. Here are a few:

The Association for Religion and Applied Behavioral Science, Bill Yon, Director, 521 North 20th St., Birmingham, Ala. 35203.

International Association of Applied Social Scientists, Steve Ruma, President, 1755 Massachusetts Ave., Washington, D.C. 20036.

The Action Training Coalition, Bill Ramsden, 1211 Chestnut St., Philadelphia, Pa. 19107.

Association for Clinical Pastoral Educators, Rev. Charles Hall, Interchurch Center, Suite 450, 475 Riverside Drive, New York, N.Y. 10027.

GROUP EXPERIENCE

The consultant with whom you decide to work should have had recent experience in working with groups in conflict. These groups may not necessarily have been church groups, but the consultant needs to have had conflict experience with voluntary associations of one kind or another. Management/labor arbitration and conflict management within hierarchical systems will not necessarily mean that the consultant knows what to expect in a church situation.

SELF-UNDERSTANDING AND PERSONAL SECURITY

You should select a person who is healthy and is aware of his own strengths and weaknesses. The person should be someone with whom you like to work. If you have some little nagging doubt in the back of your mind as to whether the consultant is "all there" himself, go on to another. There are plenty of good consultants available in metropolitan areas, and all of them have had experience at not getting a certain contract (besides, if a consultant can't take it when he is turned down, you certainly don't want him to work in your church fight).

DEMOCRATIC PHILOSOPHY

The consultant doesn't have to be a Christian to be of help to you. Indeed, there is some advantage, in terms of neutrality, if he is not. But you will want to find a person who is committed to participatory, planned-change models.[1]

APPENDIX II

Win/Lose Behavior in Competing Groups

What Happens Within Each Competing Group?

1. Each group becomes more closely knit and elicits greater loyalty from its members; members close ranks and bury some of their internal differences.
2. Group climate changes from informal, casual, playful, to work- and task-oriented; concern for members' psychological needs declines while concern for task accomplishment increases.
3. Leadership patterns tend to change from more democratic toward more autocratic; the group becomes more willing to tolerate autocratic leadership.
4. Each group becomes more highly structured and organized.
5. Each group demands more loyalty and conformity from its members in order to be able to present a "solid front."

From Edgar H. Schein, *Process Consultation: Its Role in Organization Development* (Reading, Mass., Addison-Wesley Publishing Company, Inc., 1969), pp. 72–74. Reprinted by special permission of the publisher.

What Happens Between the Competing Groups?

1. Each group begins to see the other groups as the enemy, rather than merely a neutral object.
2. Each group begins to experience distortions of perception: it tends to perceive only the best parts of itself, denying its weaknesses, and tends to perceive only the worst parts of the other group, denying its strengths. Each group is likely to develop a negative stereotype of the other ("they don't play fair the way we do.")
3. Hostility toward the other group increases while interaction and communication with the other group decreases; thus it becomes easier to maintain negative stereotypes and more difficult to correct perceptual distortions.
4. If the groups are forced into interaction—for example, if they are forced to listen to representatives plead their own and the others' cause in reference to some task— each group is likely to listen more closely to their own representative and not to listen to the representative of the other group, except to find fault with his presentation; in other words, group members tend to listen only for that which supports their own position and stereotype.

After a decision has been rendered what happens to the winner and loser?

What Happens to the Winner?

1. Winner retains its cohesion and may become even more cohesive.
2. Winner tends to release tension, lose its fighting spirit, become complacent, casual, and playful (the "fat and happy" state).
3. Winner tends toward high intragroup cooperation and concern for members' needs, and low concern for work and task accomplishment.

4. Winner tends to be complacent and to feel that winning has confirmed the positive stereotype of itself and the negative sterotype of the "enemy" group; there is little basis for reevaluating perceptions, or reexamining group operations in order to learn how to improve them.

What Happens to the Loser?

1. If the situation permits because of some ambiguity in the decision . . . , there is a strong tendency for the loser to deny or distort the reality of losing; instead, the loser will find psychological escapes like "the judges were biased," "the judges didn't really understand our solution," "the rules of the game were not clearly explained to us," "if luck had not been against us at the one key point, we would have won," and so on.
2. If the defeat is accepted, the losing group tends to splinter, unresolved conflicts come to the surface, and fights break out, all in the effort to find a cause for the loss.
3. Loser is more tense, ready to work harder, and desperate to find someone or something to blame—the leader, the group itself, the judges who decided against them, the rules of the game (the "lean and hungry" state).
4. Loser tends toward low intragroup cooperation, low concern for members' needs, and high concern for recouping by working harder.
5. Loser tends to learn a lot about itself as a group because the positive stereotype of itself and the negative stereotype of the other group are upset by the loss, forcing a reevaluation of perceptions; as a consequence, the loser is likely to reorganize and become more cohesive and effective, once the loss has been accepted realistically.

APPENDIX III

Conflict Learning
Generated by the Cities Game

In helping churchmen to understand the functions of conflict or in teaching referees the dynamics of conflict, we have often found it helpful to use simulation games of one kind or another. Many are now available commercially from a number of sources. One of the least expensive books of games and experiences is Pfeiffer and Jones, *A Handbook of Structured Experiences for Human Relations Training.*[2] Games specifically designed for church situations are available from John Knox Press and The Westminster Press. The game we like to use most often, however, is the Cities Game [3] developed by David Popov.

Since we have used this game many, many times and have developed a number of "refinements" and ways of using the experience for maximum learning, we are sharing it here to illustrate how such a game can be used, followed by a debriefing process to generate maximum learning.

Using the Cities Game in the context of training is not unlike teaching in parables. The similarity is that a story is either told (as in the parable) or acted out (as in the game) and the trainee is able to identify roles, issues, behavior, and conflict from which he might learn without the level of risk involved in actual situations.

DESCRIPTION OF THE CITIES GAME

Persons playing the game (who should number somewhere between fifteen and thirty) are divided into four
teams. The teams gather in four corners of the room and
are assigned roles. The first team is designated *Government*, the second is *Business*, the third *Slum Dwellers*, and
the fourth *Agitators*. Each team is then given what the
author calls a "Cities Poster" on which there is a sketch
of a city, depicting the various consequences for particular
actions during the course of the game. In addition to the
Cities Poster, brief instructions for the game are distributed.
Each team is then given poker chips or 3" x 5" cards representing the money capital with which its team begins the
game. Business is given $50,000; Government, $30,000;
Slum Dwellers, $10,000; and Agitators receive nothing.
Finally, each team is given a set of three ballots which will
be cast one at a time, according to the team's decision, at
various stages of the game. Each team's three ballots are in
different combinations: Business receives one ballot marked
3, one marked 1, and one marked 0. Government is given
one ballot marked 1, one marked 0, and one marked Police
Action. Slum Dwellers' ballots are marked 2, 0, and Riot.
Agitators' ballots are marked 1, 0, and Riot.

After a period of time in which each team gets ac-
quainted with the instructions, Government is given the
task of regulating the time sequences of the game. They
are: (*a*) one 5-minute period of negotiation and (*b*) a 2-
minute decision-making period in which each team makes
its decision (as a team) as to which of the three ballots it
will cast. When the ballots from the four teams are totaled,
particular consequences are called for. For example, if the
total vote is 6 or 7, with no Riot or Police Action vote,

there are rewards which are distributed (unequally, according to game rules) from the bank, which is held by a person not playing the game, to each of the four groups. In another example, if the vote total is 1, 2, or 5, or a Police Action, the consequence is that there is a tax levy and Government collects a 10-percent tax from each team.

After the consequences have been received, there follows another period of negotiation, a period of team decision-making, and a casting of the second round of ballots. The game ends after ten ballots have been cast, or when a particular set of consequences has been achieved, which in the game is called reaching the "Future City."

The energy in the game is generated as team members enter into negotiations with other teams, attempting to persuade each team to cast the ballot that will benefit the negotiators most. All kinds of promises are made and exchanged. Sometimes bribes are made (or promised) prior to the casting of a ballot.

REFLECTIONS ON SOME EXPERIENCES

When the COMMIT staff leads the Cities Game it encourages each team to define its own goal of the game. Although the instruction states that the goal of the game is to win the most money, we have encouraged each team to be creative in its interpretation of what a good goal of the game would be. Of the perceptions developed, we have seen the following four developed most frequently:

1. For one team to win the most money.
2. For all teams to reach the Future City with a fairly equal distribution of wealth.
3. Some teams have seen as their goal the playing out of a role without relationship to either money or

the Future City consequences of the way they play the role. This is most often true of the Agitators, who find their goal to be merely agitation.

4. Conflict, or "the fun of playing," becomes a goal for some people. They enjoy the generation and expression of all kinds of energy in the running around, loud talk, wheeling and dealing.

It is very interesting to see, during the process of the game, how the room is very quickly filled with loud laughter, frantic running around, secretive conferences in various corners of the room. There is strategy development, threats are exchanged, and there is usually a great deal of involvement among the players. Among the more typical kinds of behavior to observe are:

1. The ways in which people make commitments, then break them when it is to their advantage to do so.
2. How coalitions among various groups develop—specifically (and most often), between the Agitators and the Slum Dwellers on the one hand, and Business and Government on the other, as they see that it is to their advantage to plan mutual strategies.
3. How cheating is perceived to be acceptable in order to win the goal that a player or team has selected.
4. The way the players move around the room and cluster at points where serious (and often loud) negotiation is going on, and the way in which there is loud cheering and booing as the results of the ballots cast are revealed. These all indicate a very high degree of personal participation, role identification, and involvement in an intense group experience.

Among the more extreme actions we have experienced during the course of the Cities Game have been actual mild violence among the players, such as ganging up on key holdouts. We have also experienced bank robberies in which members of the Agitators or Slum Dwellers came up to the person who was holding the money, grabbed the money, ran off with it, and then announced a bank robbery. This caused anger and consternation on the part of the others. There have been, on other occasions, coalitions developed between Business, Slum Dwellers, and Agitators for the purpose of overthrowing and replacing Government. If Government did not capitulate, they would declare the money system to be void and proceed to issue new currency, using paper out of notebooks, etc., and thus establish alternate governmental processes. On one occasion when the Cities Game involved a group of seminary students, they kidnapped and held as hostage one of the members of Government while negotiations were going on.

Because Government is in control of enforcing the various time periods, it is frequently their practice to shorten or lengthen time periods according to where they are in their negotiations. We have found that if we allow a total of two hours to play the game, we rarely either complete the ten moves or reach the Future City, because of manipulation of time periods by Government.

DESCRIPTION OF DEBRIEFING AND REFLECTION

When the game is called to a halt, we spend at least another hour in a debriefing and reflection process. We do this with all the players together and will conduct the debriefing and reflection session in various ways, depending upon the particular kind of learning appropriate for the training process where the game is used. It takes a strong leader in the debriefing to get the group to focus on the reflection process. Often the groups will wish to continue discussing the game, describing strategies, laughing about particular instances, and retelling stories in such a way as to indicate clearly how closely identified they remain with the role they played. It is difficult for them, at least in the early part of the debriefing, to extract themselves from that role in order to look at the processes of the game for learning purposes.

We have indicated below several areas for discussion which can profitably be explored at the end of the game and which will indicate the variety of learning that can develop:

1. *Leadership roles.* Leadership roles can be looked at in terms of observing how certain individuals emerged as leaders and other people assumed the role of follower. Discovering the ways in which persons were able to be persuasive and influential is an important learning experience for all.

2. *Use of power.* The use of power is also another way that learning can be generated as a result of the experience. For example, the questions could be asked:

    How was authority used?

    How was influence used?

    How was coercion used?

    What was the power of the man who had a vision out of which developed a clear sense of goals and strategies, as over against the person who had no vision and no clarity about the direction in which his behavior was moving?

3. *The game plays you.* It becomes fairly clear that people who have known each other for a long time suddenly discover that they are interreacting in entirely new ways, consistent with their perception of the role that the game has assigned to them. We have named this kind of behavior "the game is playing you." In other words, the system in which they are operating determines the kind of behavior for

the players. Of course people say, "I was only playing a game," or "I was only acting as I understood
Agitators are supposed to act." Our response is
usually to point out that, nonetheless, they behaved
in such a way as to act out their perception of what
their role required. This is important learning in
terms of grasping and understanding the behavior of
other persons; one learns to ask, What kind of game
do people understand themselves to be involved in?
This generates their perception of their role and
therefore their type of behavior.

4. *Organizing skills.* Much time can be profitably
spent looking at the ability of various people to
organize others in common action, or looking back
on the course of the game to see what the points
were on which group action was organized, and to
attempt to analyze the process whereby group action
was developed. When playing this game with a
group of people in a training design that called for
the learning of community organization skills, we
interrupted the game at the end of three votes. We
asked each person to reflect on the kinds of organizing that had been done and the kinds that needed
to be done in order to accomplish the goals that
had been chosen. After the people had ten minutes
to work on their own, the game was again picked up
at the point where it had been interrupted. The
players then attempted to implement a self-conscious
organizing strategy within the game.

5. *Relevance to theology.* When playing this Cities
Game with seminary students or clergy we have, on
occasion, after six rounds of ballot-casting, declared
the Sabbath Day and asked each of the men to try
to take himself out of the role he has assumed in the
game. In its place he was to take the role of a
pastor who is preparing a sermon to be delivered

to a congregation made up of all the other people in the room (in the roles they had assumed during the course of the game). We also suggested that they think of other ways in which the church's presence could provide an intervention (on behalf of the church's goal) into the game-created society in that room.

6. *Conflict management.* Three particular kinds of conflict are often experienced during the course of the game around which reflection processes might be organized:

   a. *Role conflict.* By this we mean the conflict experienced within any one player as he tries to determine behavior consistent with the role he has been assigned and the way in which he chooses to relate that role behavior to his understanding of ethical behavior. It is interesting that during the debriefing and reflection processes people will frequently report feelings of anxiety and guilt in relation to particular kinds of behavior they had used during the game. In fact, treating someone in a way that betrays humanness, even in a game situation, produces guilt. This is usually manifested in confessions of unethical behavior which the player has to get off his chest. In addition, it is interesting to note how people understand the role they have been assigned in the game to be a license to practice types of behavior that they say they would not utilize in any other kind of life experience.

   It is only seldom that we have witnessed players in the game choosing self-conscious ethical stances, out of which they play their role. One vivid example was witnessed as we used this Cities Game with a group of entering freshman at Claremont College in Pomona, California. One of the freshmen chose to understand his role, which happened to be that of a businessman, to be framed within his understanding of ethical behavior. He is an articulate and persuasive young man and was able to convince his other business team members that it was in their long-range self-interest to behave openly, honestly, and in such a manner as to see that the goal of the Future City would be of mutual benefit to all players of the game. In order to win the confidence of his teammates and that of the other teams, he used a collaborative mode wherein he explained to everyone how business would give up the making of large profits and would, in fact, distribute the wealth it had. This was a vivid example of the player choosing to play the game rather than letting the game play him, to use the expression employed earlier.

Often people find that it is really fun to lie, cheat, and steal when they see that it serves their own self-interest and that the game provides a license for that kind of behavior. This is especially true for the Agitators who see that there is very little to lose by such behavior in the context of the game. They begin with no money and can generate power only by threat or by casting "Riot" votes and other forms of agitation. However, a good deal of conversation and learning can develop when a part of the reflection process is focused on the relation between the conflict which people experienced and the role they were assigned.

b. *Team conflict.* This is most often generated around the struggle for leadership and the development of team goals and strategies. It can be an especially strong and vivid conflict if two normally strong leaders in a group arrive at opposing understandings of the goal and the strategy for accomplishing it. Sometimes the result of conflict will cause the person who finally loses leadership to drop out of the game or (as is sometimes pointed out) to assume a role akin to that of the hippie dropout from society. Particular kinds of learning made possible by looking at this team conflict have to do with helping people understand how they behave in high-tension conflict and confrontation situations.

c. *Conflict strategies between teams.* Another very helpful type of learning (particularly for white suburban middle-class training groups) is to discover that it is possible and sometimes necessary to develop strategies of conflict in order to reach certain goals. In our training processes we normally designate three basic forms of strategy: collaboration, campaign, and conflict, which we learned from Rolland Warren.

> (1) Collaboration strategies are used in situations where all those involved understand and agree with the kind of change that is needed. The organizer's task is merely to mobilize people for that change.

> (2) Campaign strategies are those which are utilized when the change team clearly understands that all the people involved would agree with the necessity of change if they understood the facts. Therefore, a strategy of education and a campaign

to communicate all the facts is developed.

(3) Conflict strategies are those in which the change team understands that it is contrary to the self-interest of a number of people (or structures) in a given situation to participate in the system or in the change processes. Therefore, if the change is to occur, it is necessary for the team to enter into conflict (the object of which is to overpower, or to outvote, or in other ways remove from the field of concern the obstructive forces preventing change). It is to be assumed that those in the church have a preference for strategies of collaboration and campaign and an aversion to strategies of conflict. If it is the case that in white middle-class America there is a norm of collaboration and campaign that may be described as a theological commitment or a cultural norm, one needs to ask in what realms of behavior this norm applies. It is clear that a free-enterprise economic system places positive value on the conflict strategy, particularly if its use leads to success.

Any form of training for community organization needs to make the trainees aware of the importance of looking at all strategy options (including conflict) in order that the change team can select the most appropriate and creative strategy. A good deal of conversation and learning has been generated in the Cities Game in the area of conflict strategies.

Conclusions

In the urban training that we have done at COMMIT, we include the Cities Game, or other such games, in early phases of the training process. We see this as a kind of team-building experience which provides intense common experience for a new group of trainees. It often becomes a paradigm experience that the group uses in measuring the involvement and excitement of its own groups. It is an intensive training experience in that it calls for full participation, for interaction, and for a good measure of reflection and conversation about concrete behavior. In addition, the procedures help us in training groups in the processes of reflection that are critical to the ongoing development of social change processes. Those who are unable to reflect (with some skill and sensitivity) on their game experiences usually have the greatest difficulty increasing their skills and changing their behavior.

One further reflection warning: The Cities Game is in no way a substitute for direct involvement of the group in the life of the metropolis. If one intends to have a grasp of the reality of an agitator or a slum dweller, business or government, one must spend time in the actual world with those who live, move, and have their being in that world.

Design of a Training Event for Referees

GOALS:

To develop in each participant the skills needed in conflict management and resolution.

To develop functional teams with next-step action plans for conference, association, and local church conflict management.

To work workable conflict present in the group either for conference, association, or local church settings.

OBJECTIVES: Increase basic knowedge of behavioral science theory relevant to conflict management and group life.

Increase knowledge (cognitive and affective) of how each individual operates in conflict situations.

Increase knowledge (cognitive and affective) of the dynamics of groups in conflict.

Increase knowledge of instruments available for analyzing and factoring conflict situations.

Increase knowledge of intervention strategies for managing conflict:
    third-party consultation
    use of self
    use of groups
Develop next-step action plans for the various conflict management teams.

SCHEDULE: Friday evening, 7:30
    Introductions
    Getting acquainted with each other
    Getting acquainted with myself as a conflict manager (self-assessment exercise)
    Developing learning goals for the weekend
Saturday
    9:00 A.M.
        Behavioral science input
        Simulation of conflict situation
    Noon
        Lunch
    1:00 P.M.
        Continue simulation
        Debrief simulation
    6:00 P.M.
        Supper
    7:30 P.M.
        Input on third-party intervention strategies
Sunday
    9:00 A.M.
        Input on analyzing and factoring conflict
        Developing next-step plans
    Noon
        Lunch

NOTES

1. These categories were suggested by Gordon Lipitt in Ch. 15 of his book *Organizational Renewal* (Appleton-Century-Crofts, 1969).

2. J. William Pfeiffer and John Jones, *A Handbook of Structured Experiences for Human Relations Training*, Vol. III (Iowa City, Iowa: University Associates Press, 1970).

3. David Popov, "The Cities Game," *Psychology Today*, Nov., 1968.

Bibliography

Argyris, Chris, *Intervention Theory and Method: A Behavioral Science View*. Addison-Wesley Publishing Company, Inc., 1970.

Beckhard, Richard, *Organization Development: Strategies and Models*. Addison-Wesley Publishing Company, Inc., 1969.

Berne, Eric, *Principles of Group Treatment*. Grove Press, Inc., 1966.

———— *The Structure and Dynamics of Organizations and Groups*. Grove Press, Inc., 1963.

———— *Transactional Analysis in Psychotherapy*. Grove Press, Inc., 1961.

Coser, Lewis, *The Functions of Social Conflict*. The Free Press, 1956.

De Boer, John, *Let's Plan: A Guide to the Planning Process for Voluntary Organizations*. Pilgrim Press, 1970.

Dittes, James E., *The Church in the Way*. Charles Scribner's Sons, 1967.

Fordyce, Jack K., and Weil, Raymond, *Managing with People: A Manager's Handbook of Organization Development Methods*. Addison-Wesley Publishing Company, Inc., 1971.

Harris, Thomas, *I'm OK—You're OK: A Practical Guide to Transactional Analysis*. Harper & Row, Publishers, Inc., 1969.

Lee, Robert, and Galloway, Russell, *The Schizophrenic Church: Conflict Over Community Organization*. The Westminster Press, 1969.

Lippitt, Ronald; Watson, Jeanne; and Westley, Bruce, *The Dynamics of Planned Change: A Comparative Study of Principles and Techniques*. Harcourt, Brace and Company, Inc., 1958.

Maier, Norman, *Problem-Solving Discussions and Conferences*. McGraw-Hill Book Co., Inc., 1963.

Nylen, Donald; Mitchell, J. Robert; and Stout, Anthony, *Handbook of Staff Development and Human Relations Training: Materials Developed for Use in Africa*. National Education Association of the United States, 1967.

Schaller, Lyle E., *The Local Church Looks to the Future*. Abingdon Press, 1968.

———— *Parish Planning, How to Get Things Done in Your Church*. Abingdon Press, 1971.

Schein, Edgar H., *Process Consultation: Its Role in Organization Development*. Addison-Wesley Publishing Company, Inc., 1969.

Tannenbaum, Robert; Weschler, Irving R.; and Massarik, Fred, *Leadership and Organization: A Behavioral Science Approach*. McGraw-Hill Book Co., Inc., 1961.